Passover Coloring Book

The Passover Story in Pictures – Joseph, Moses, Egypt, Pharaoh, Plagues – Pesach Coloring For Kids

Rachel Mintz

Images used under license from Shutterstock.com

Copyright © 2018 Palm Tree Publishing - All rights reserved.
No part of this publication may be reproduced, distributed, or transmitted in any form or by any means, including photocopying, recording, or other electronic or mechanical methods, without the prior written permission of the publisher, except in the case of brief quotations embodied in critical reviews and certain other noncommercial uses permitted by copyright law.

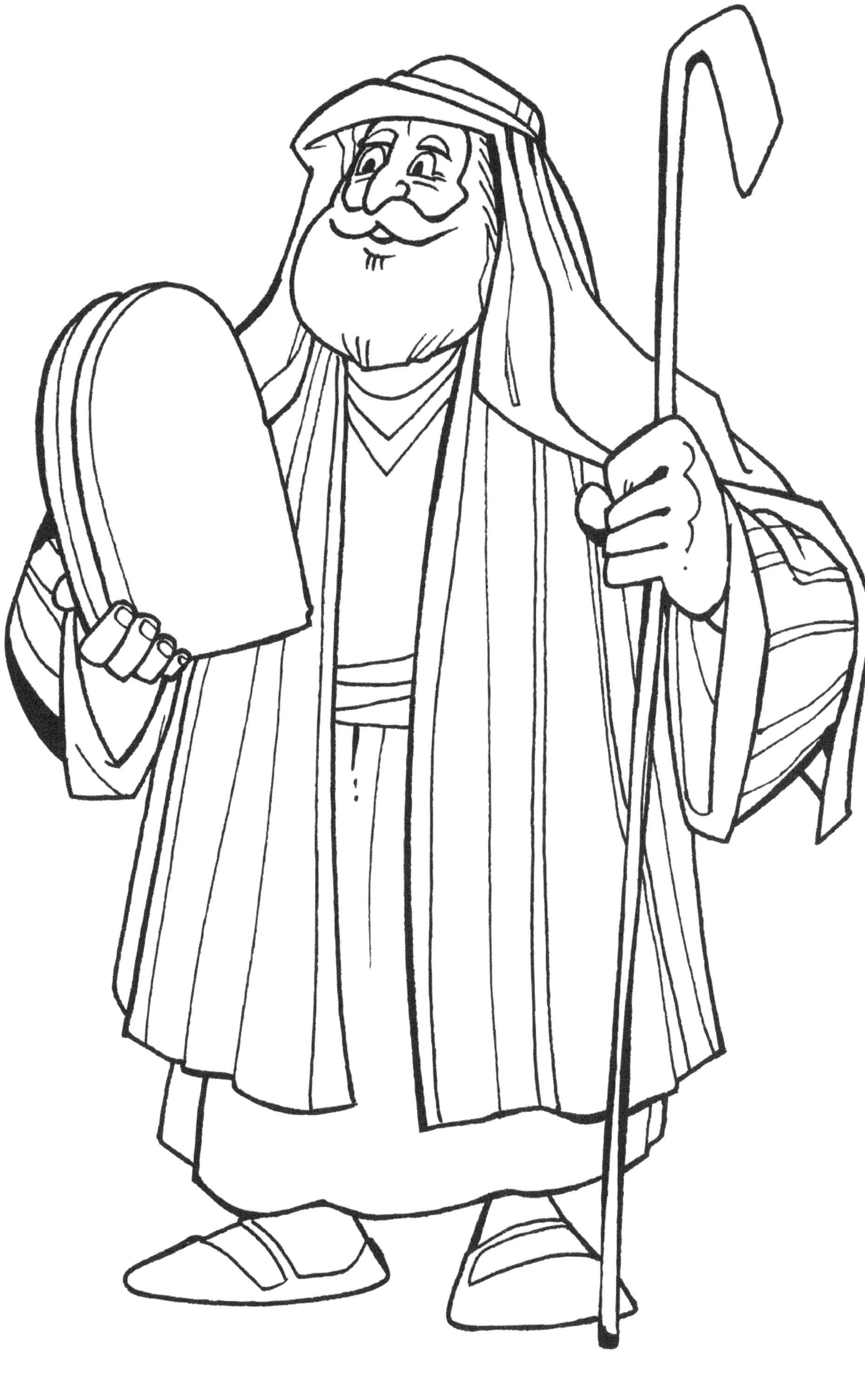

Jacob sends his ten sons to Egypt, because of the famine.

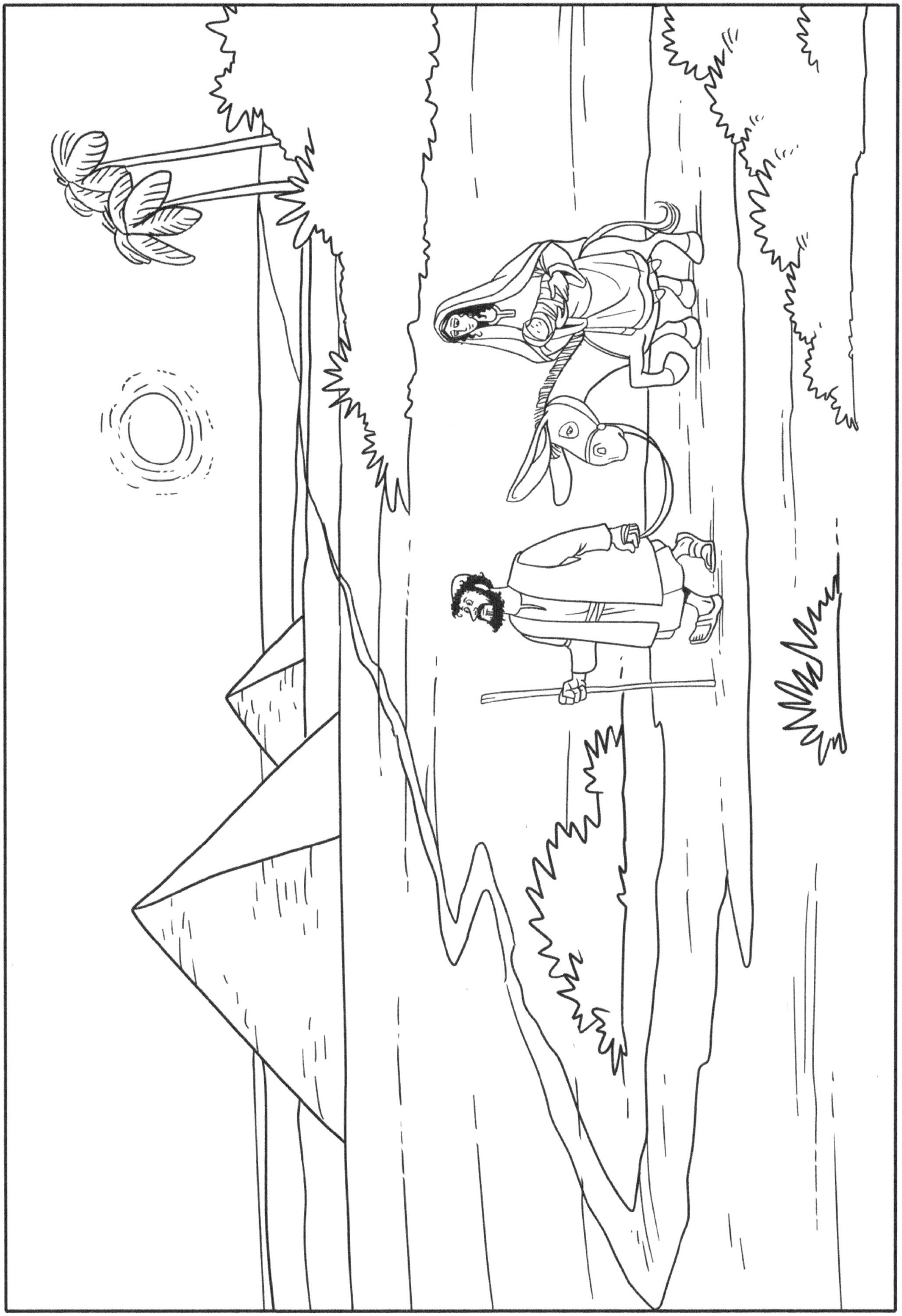

Joseph is in Egypt

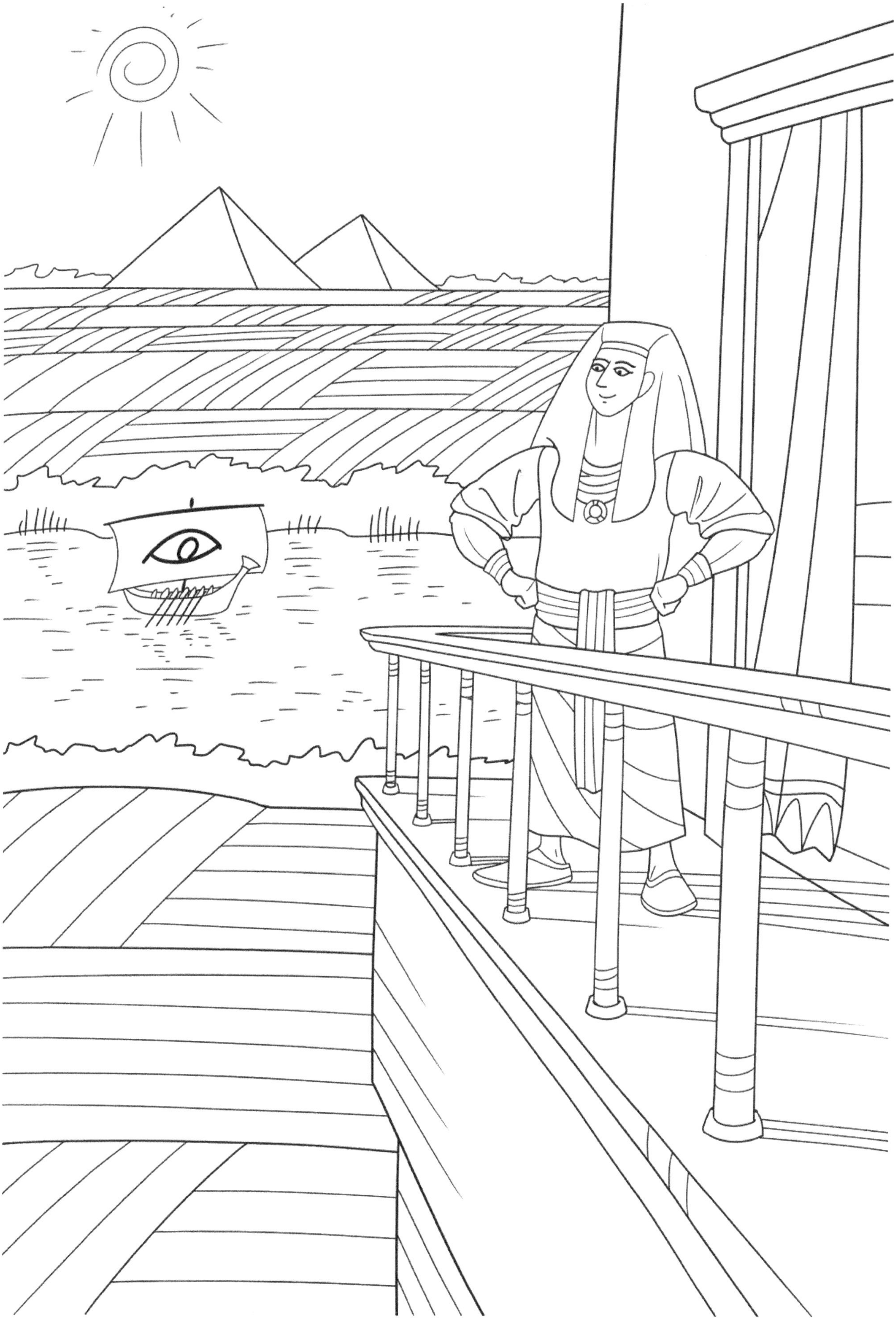

Joseph knows how to interpret Pharaoh's dreams about the seven thin cows.

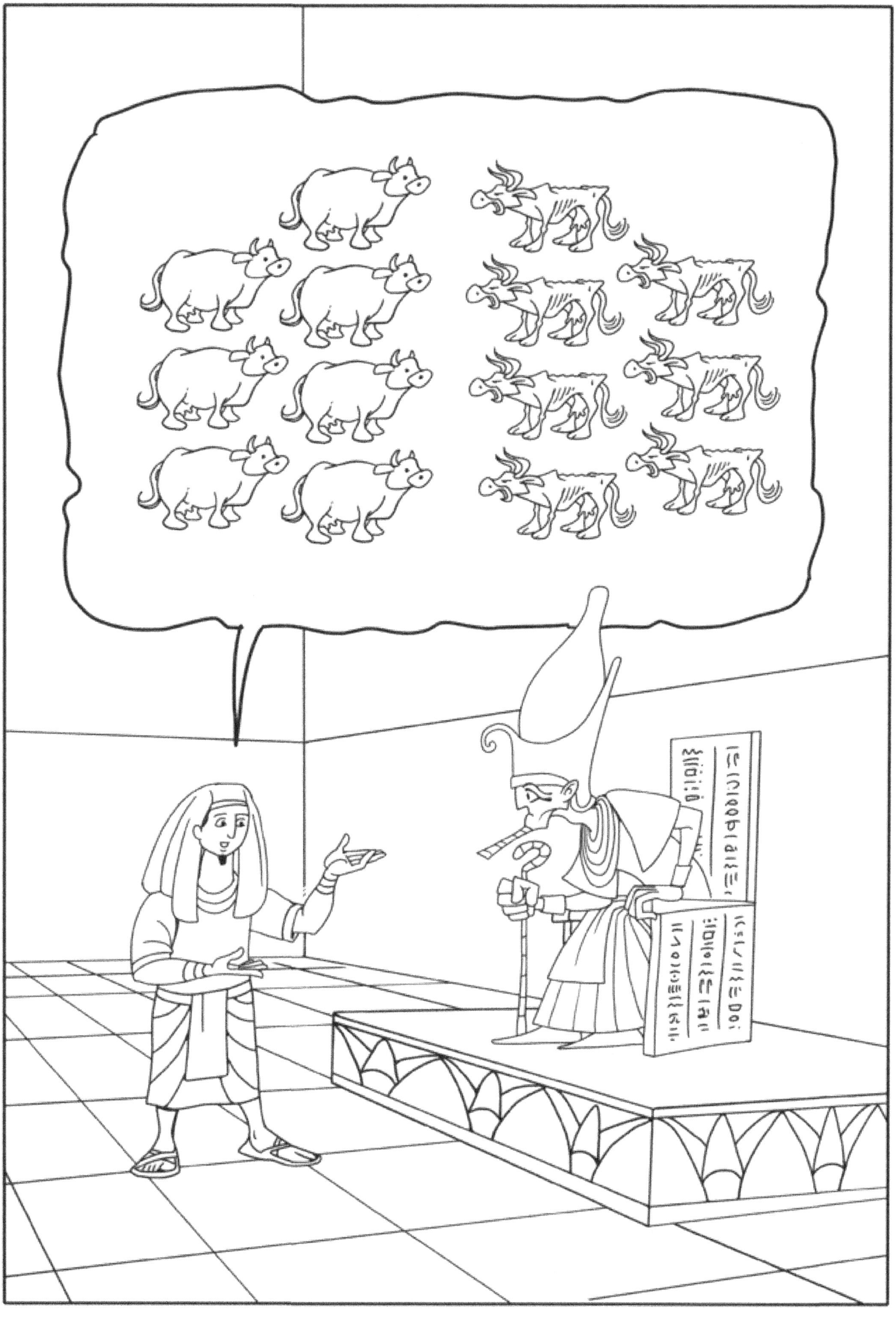

But years later, came a new king and the people of Israel were enslaved by the new Pharaoh.

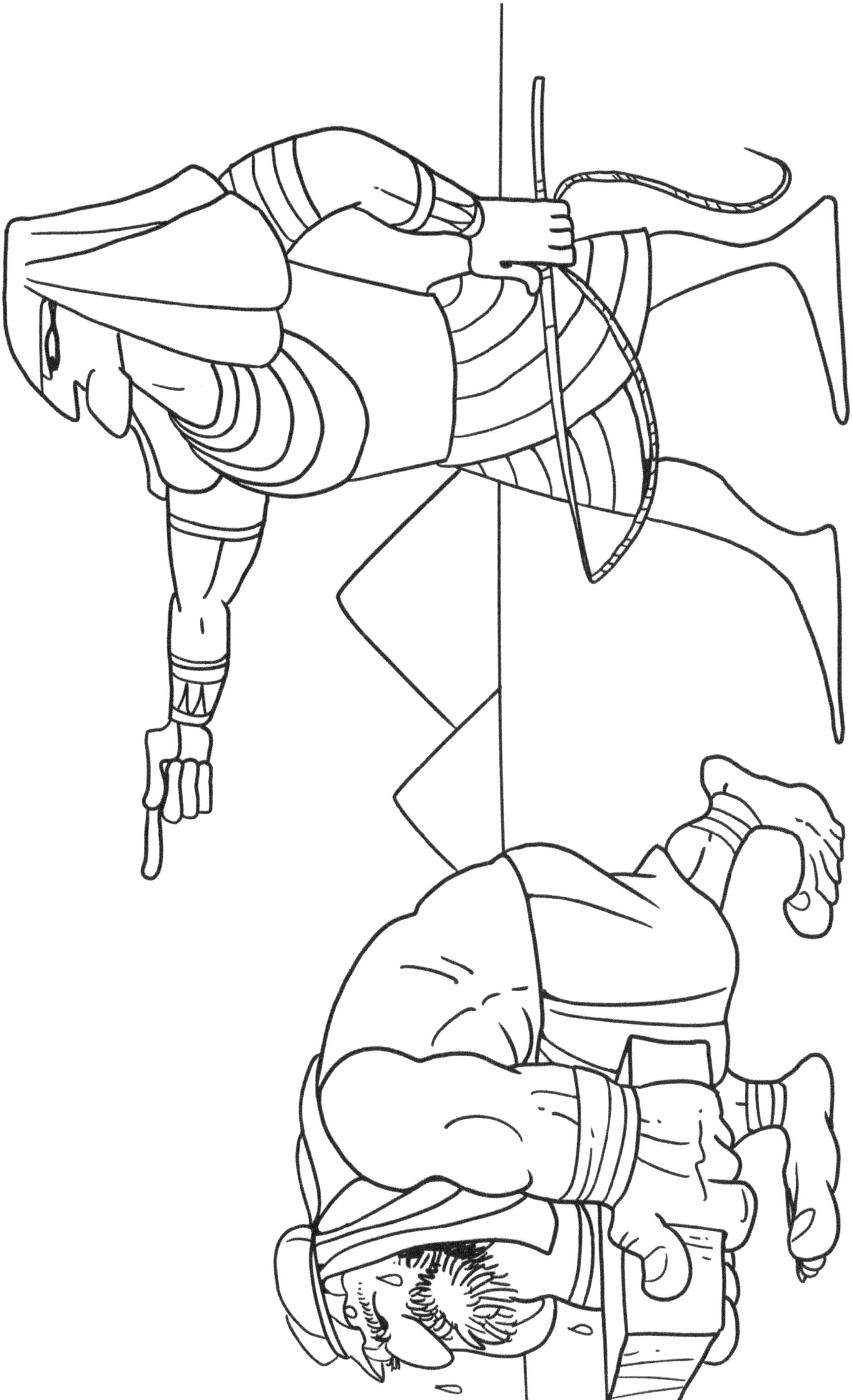

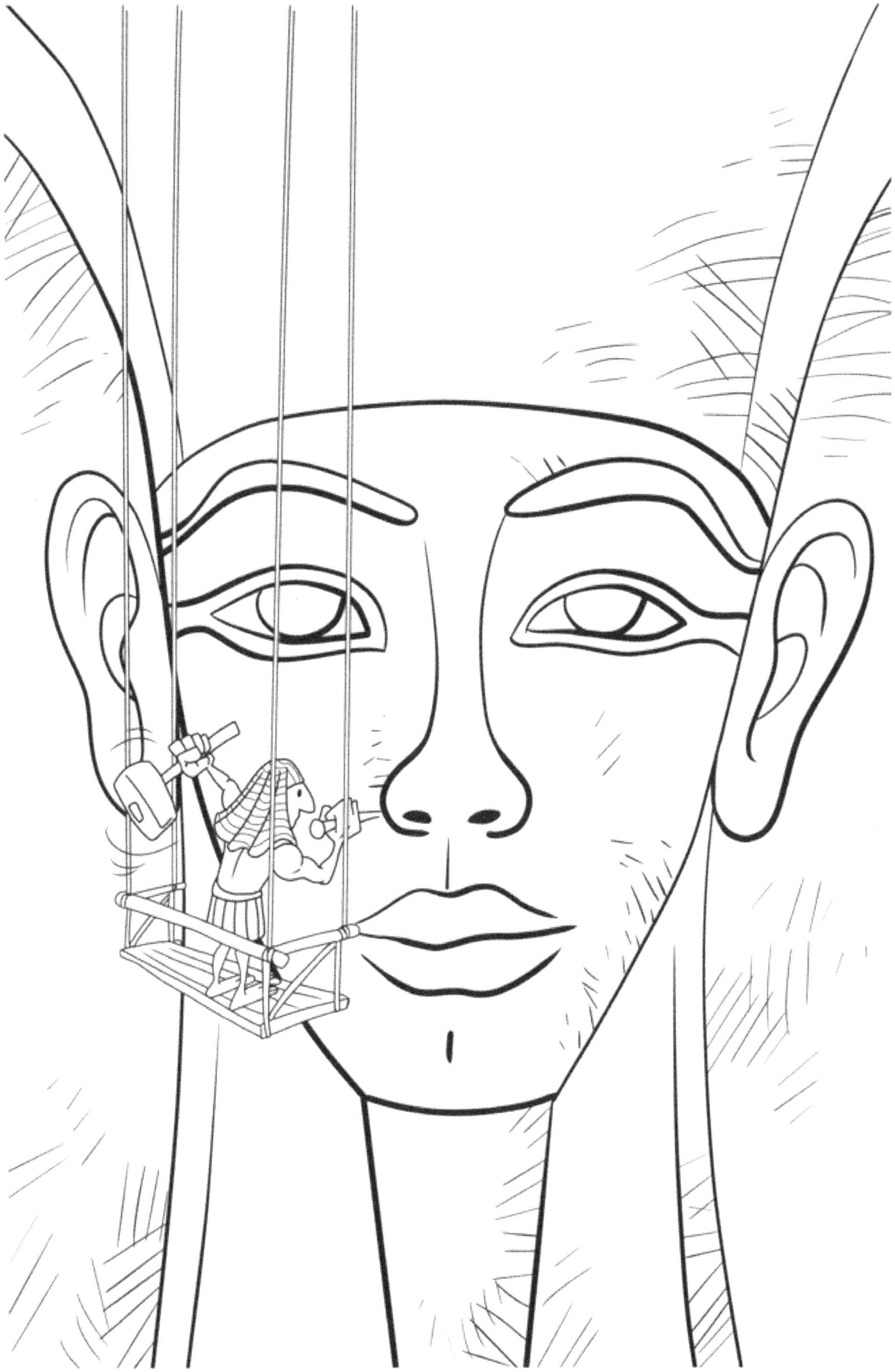

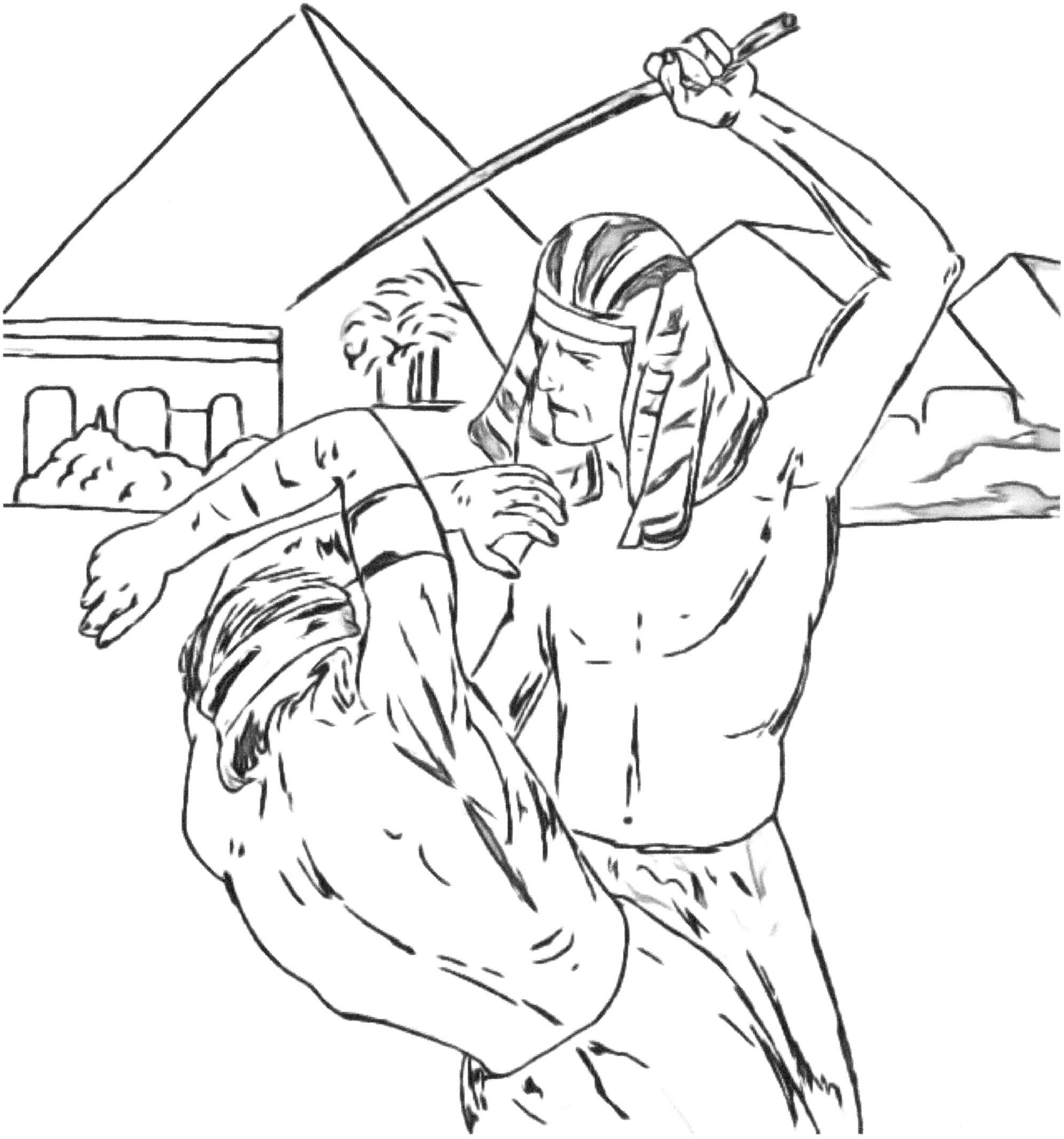

Pharaoh commands that all the newborn males will be thrown into the Nile! Moses is placed in a small basket. His sister Miriam hides among the bushes to watch over her little brother.

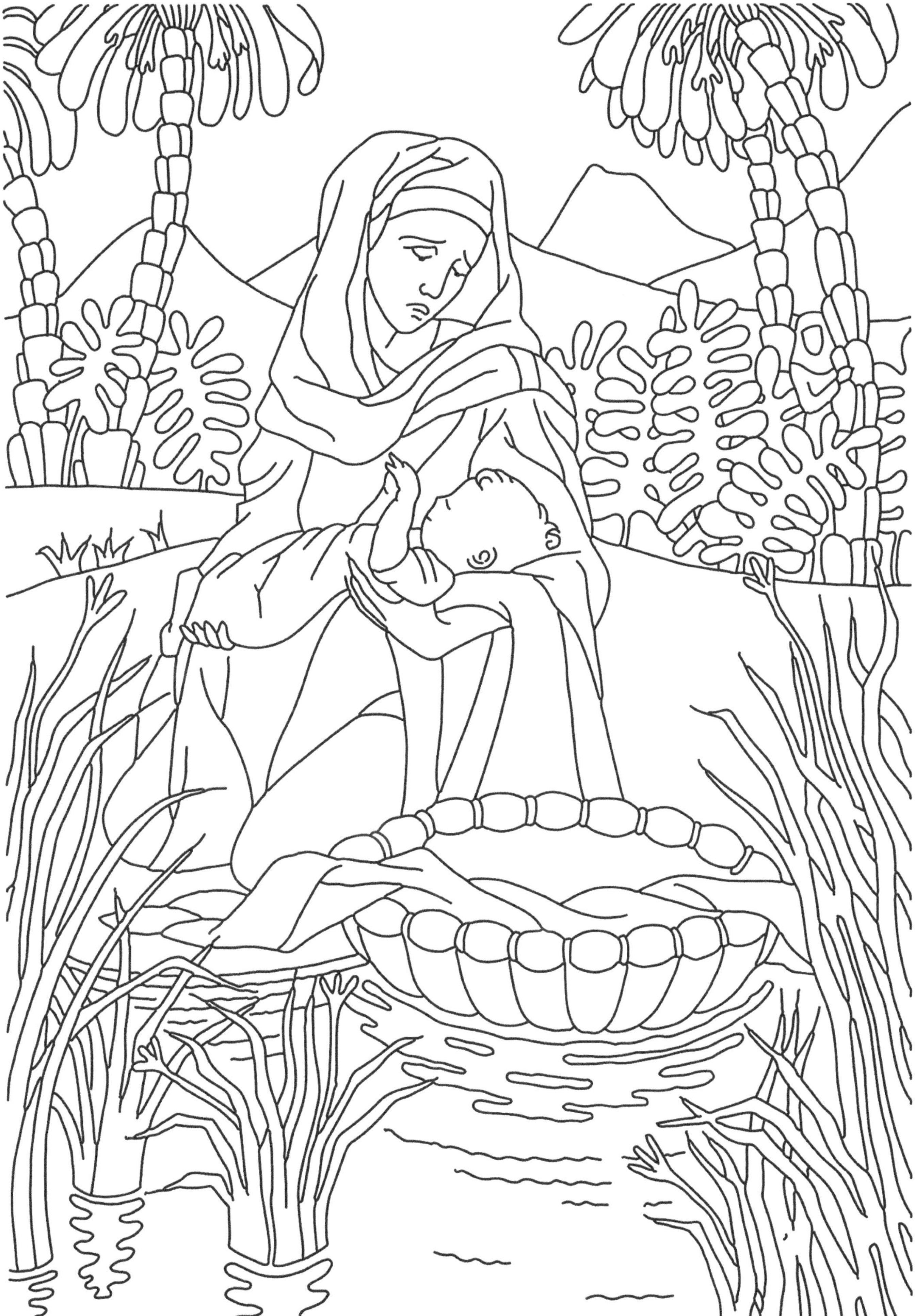

Pharaoh's daughter comes to bath in the Nile, and sees the floating cradle in the water. She takes Moses back to the palace and he is raised as Prince of Egypt.

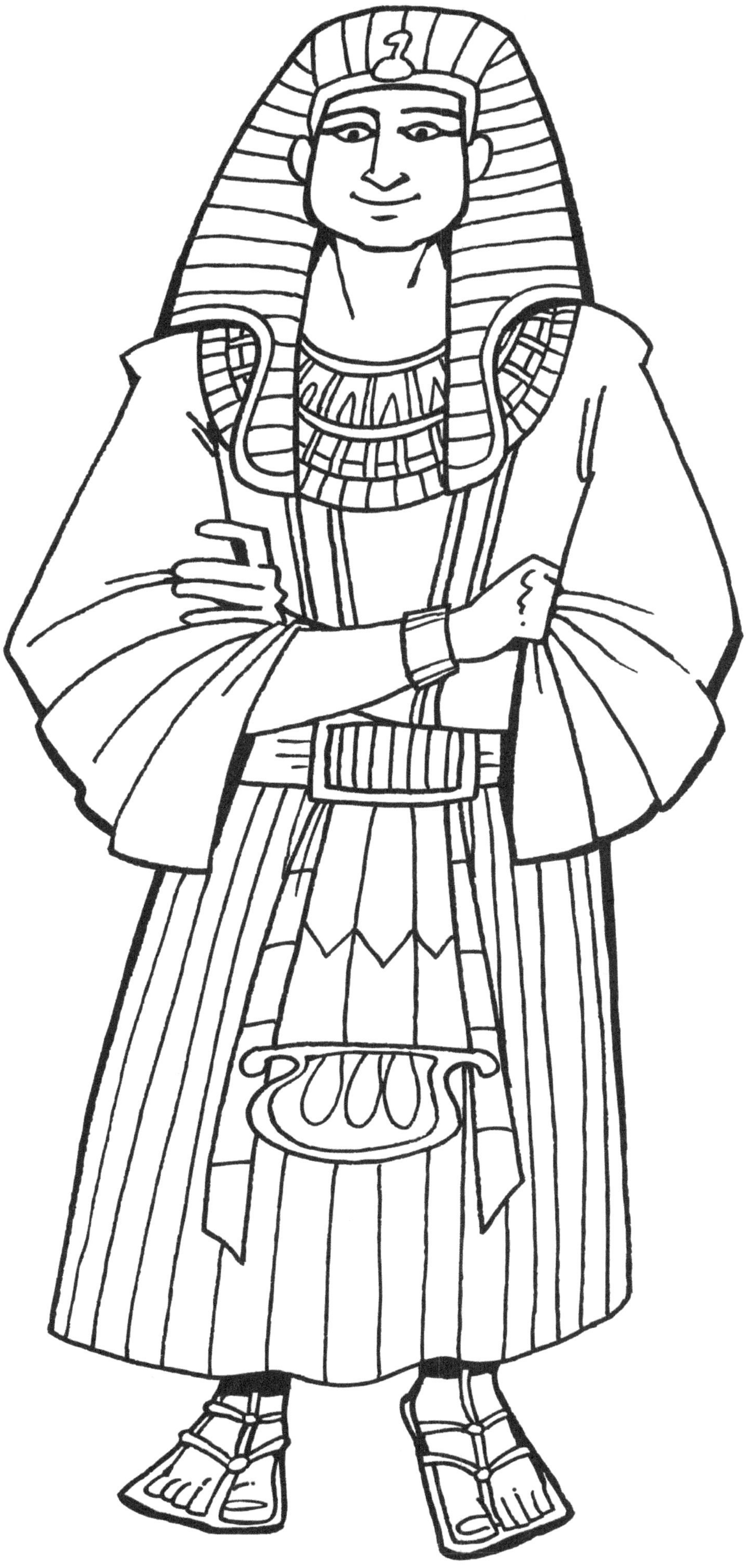

One day Moses sees an Egyptian guard hitting one of the Children of Israel. He attacks the guard and flees into the desert.

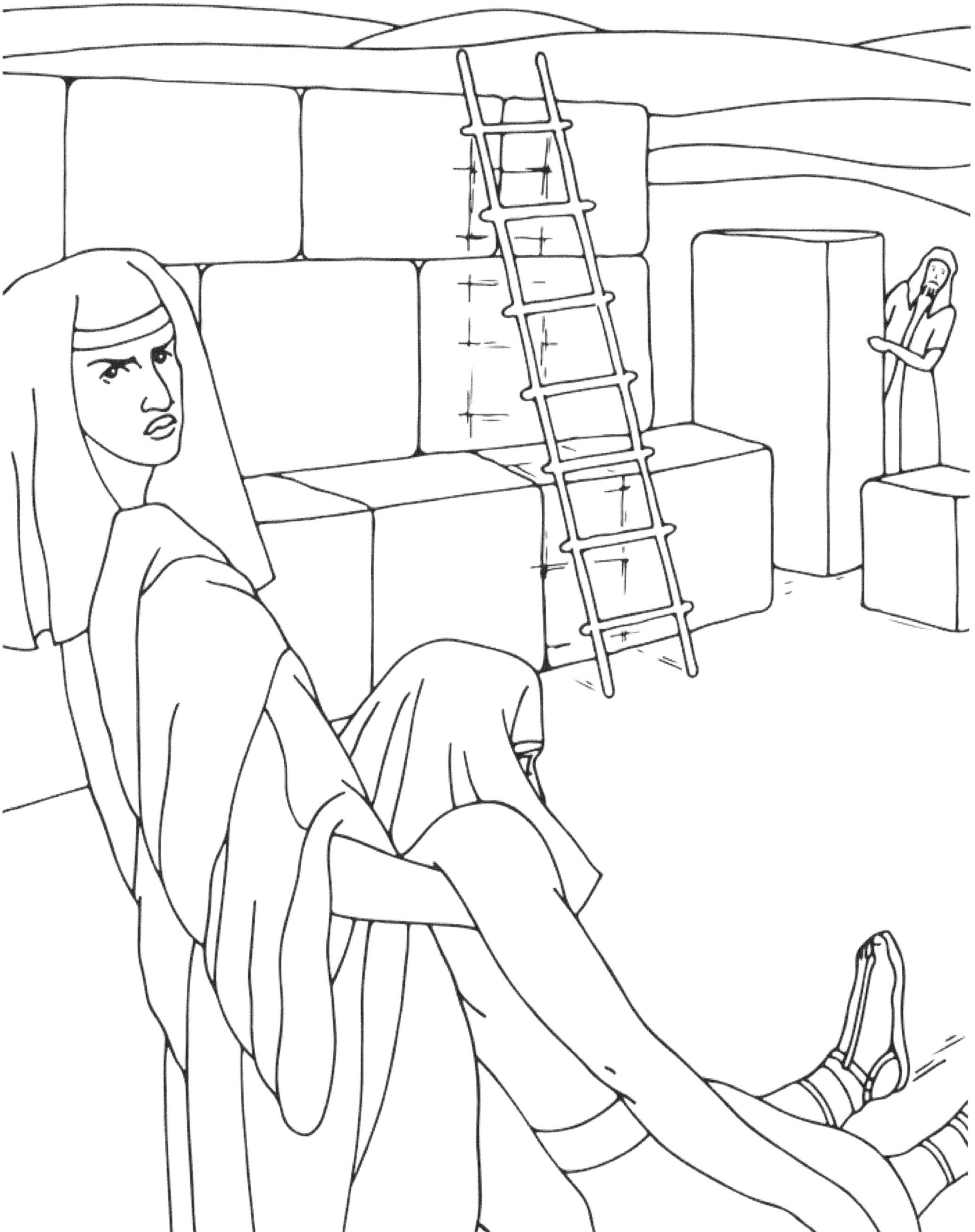

There he sees the burning bush! God tells Moses to go back to Egypt and lead the Children of Israel back home.

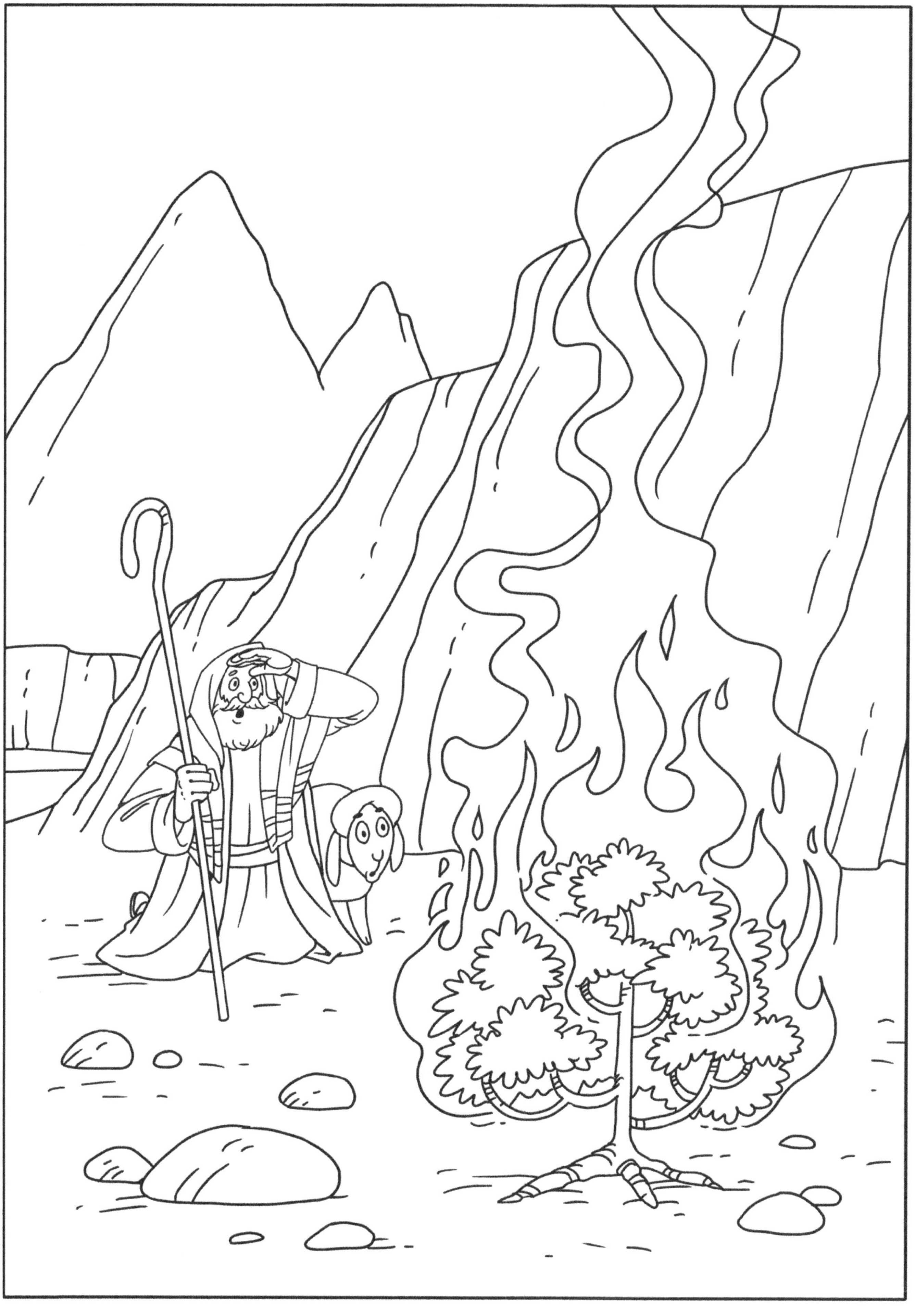

Let My People Go! Moses demands pharaoh to free the Children of Israel. But the Egyptian king does not let go. God sends a series of Ten plagues on the Egyptians.

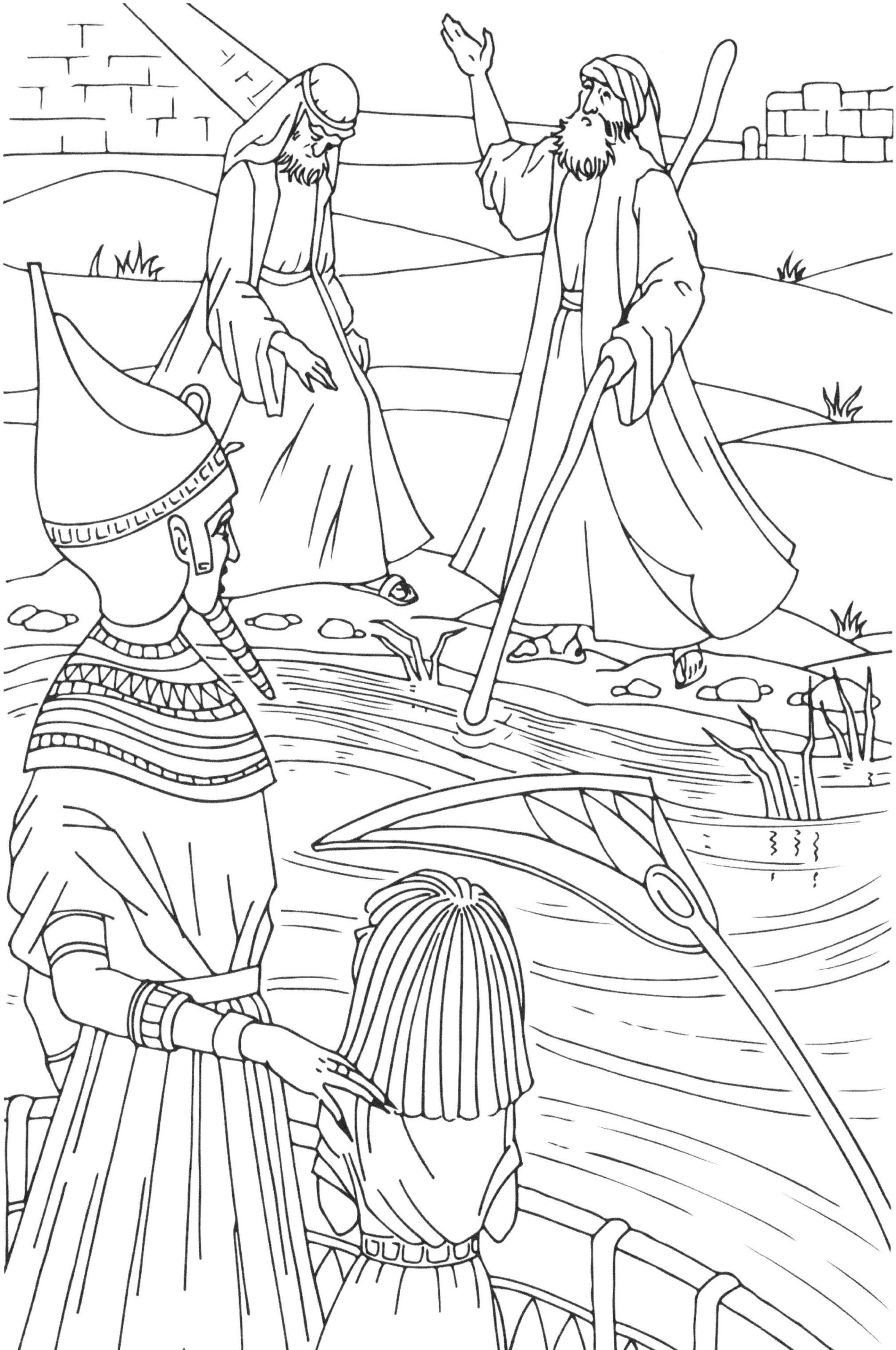

The Nile water are turning into blood!

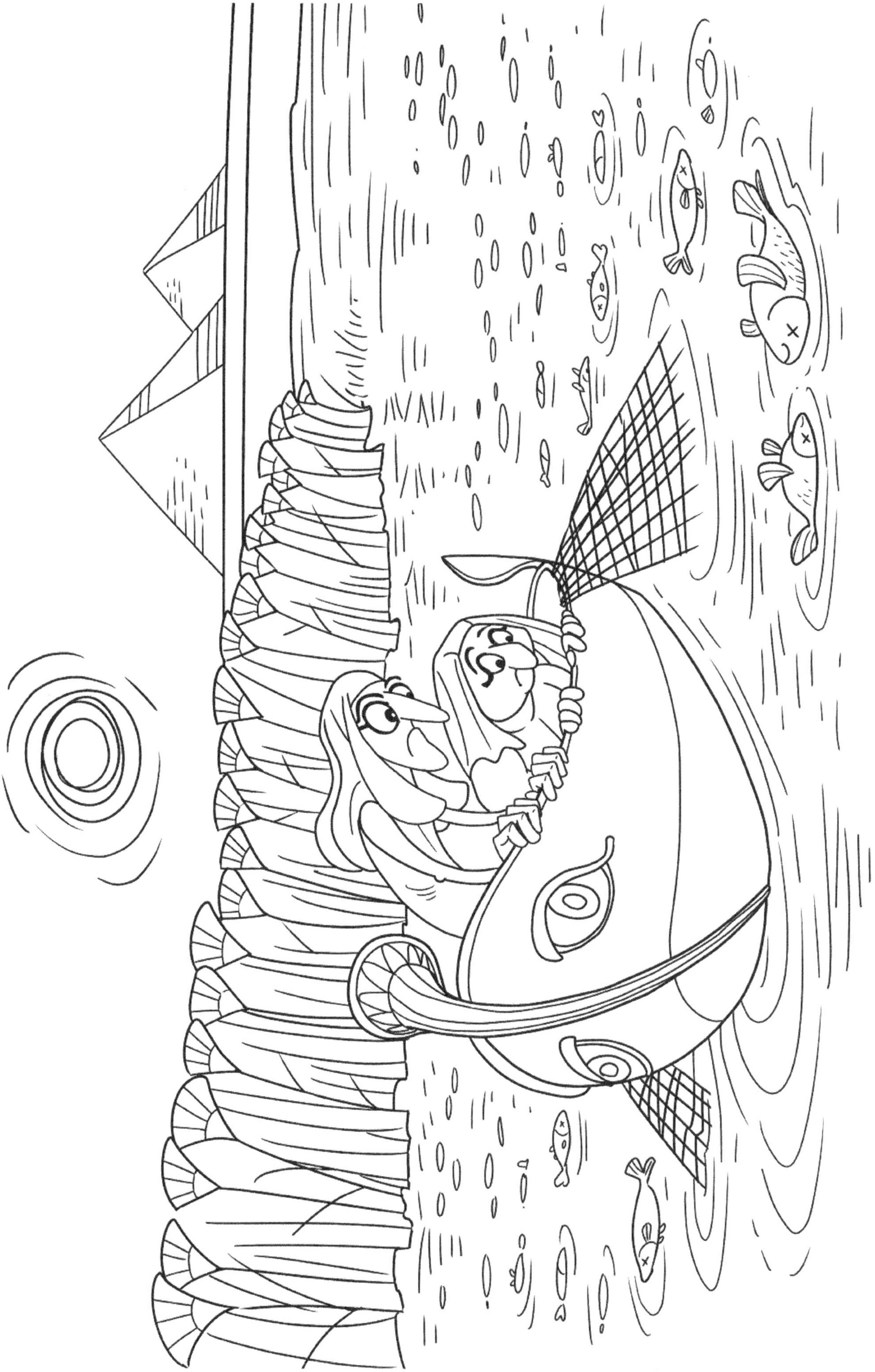

Pharaoh refuses to let go of the People of Israel. So more plagues are coming. Frogs swarm across the kings palace. Then Lice.

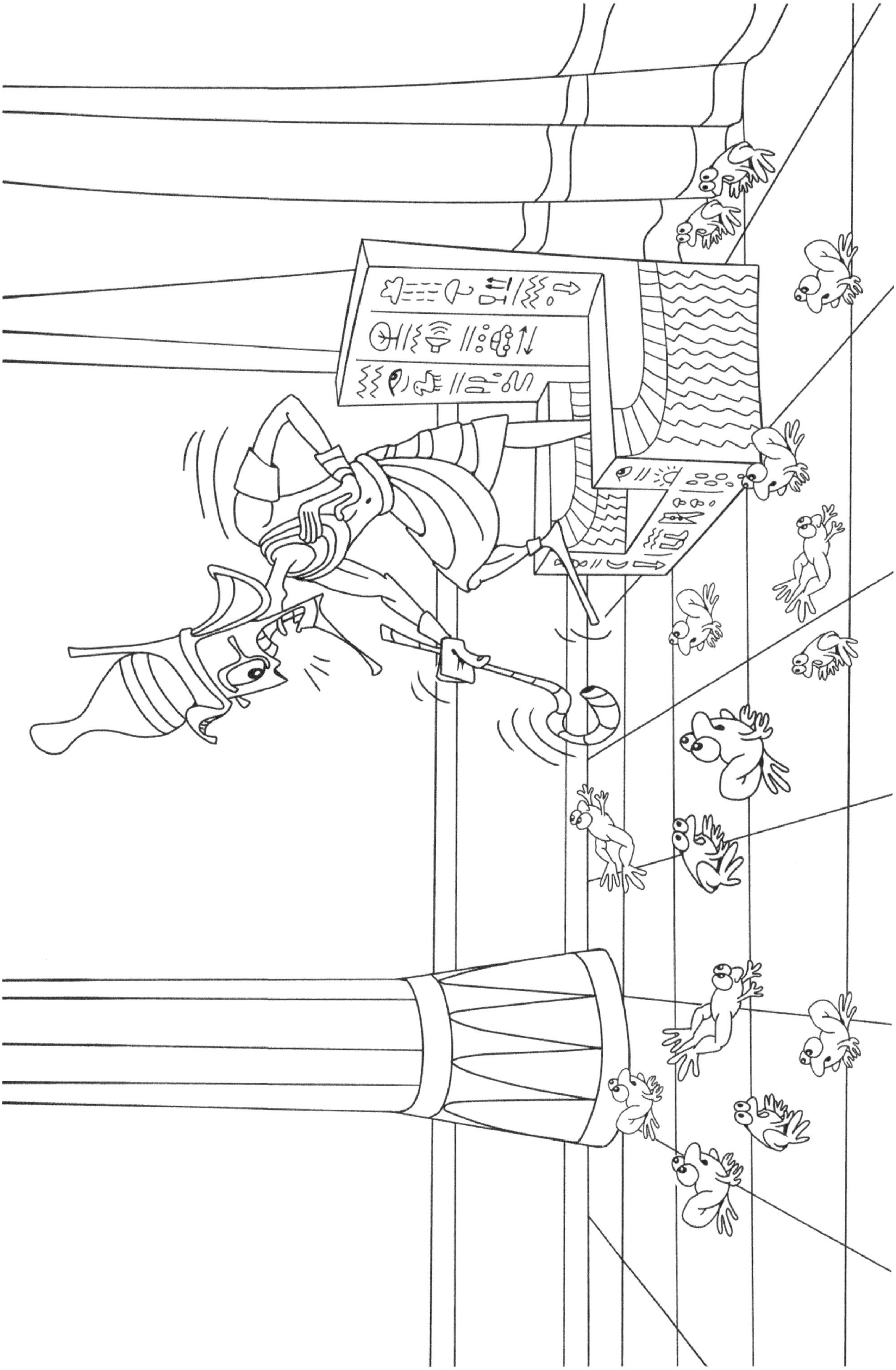

Wild beasts! Then the domestic animals are killed! Then Boils! Then Hail of fire and ice. Then swarm of locusts! And pitch Darkness.

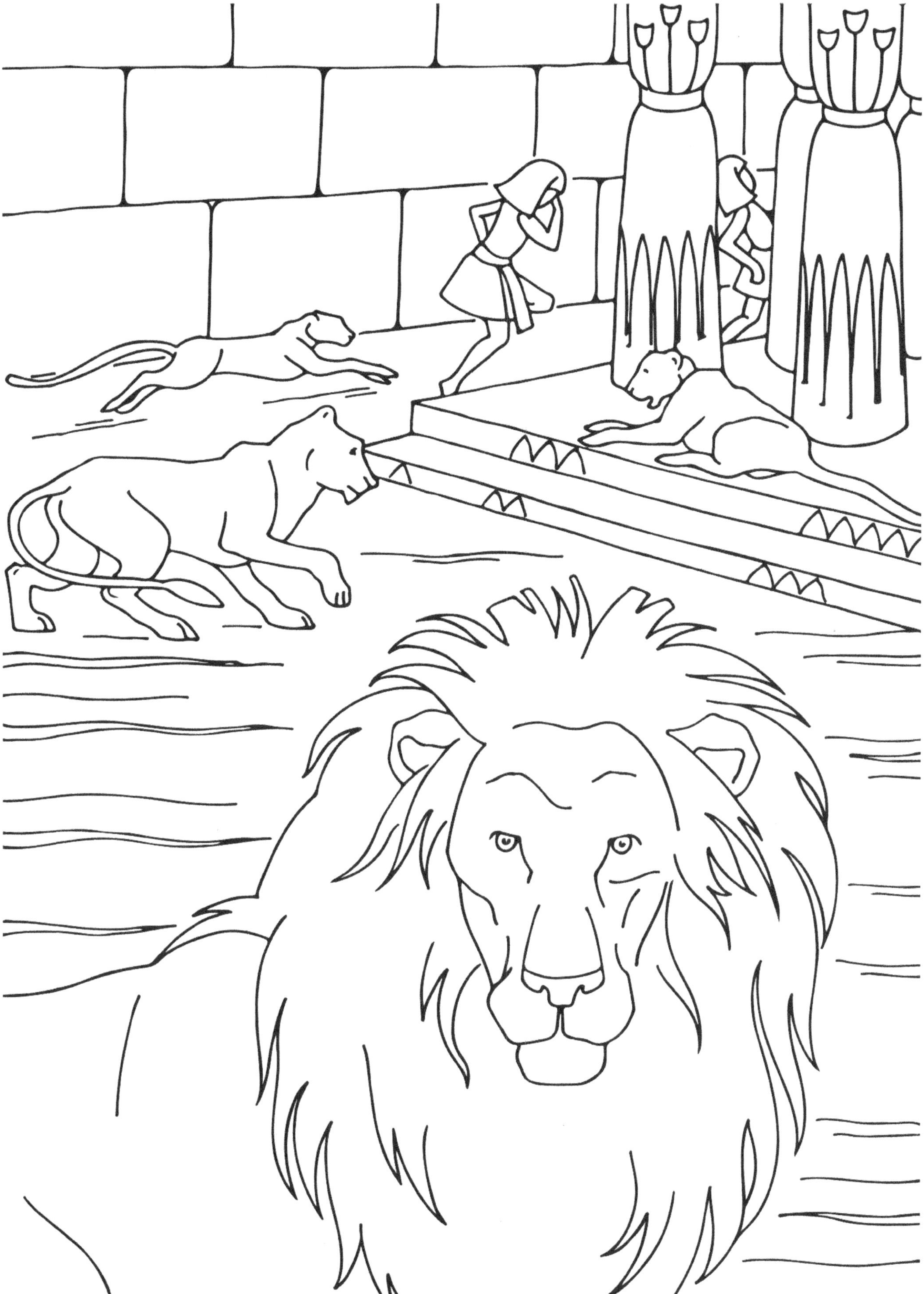

God orders the Israelites to smear blood on the doorposts of their homes, so he can PASS-OVER their homes when he strikes the Egyptians.

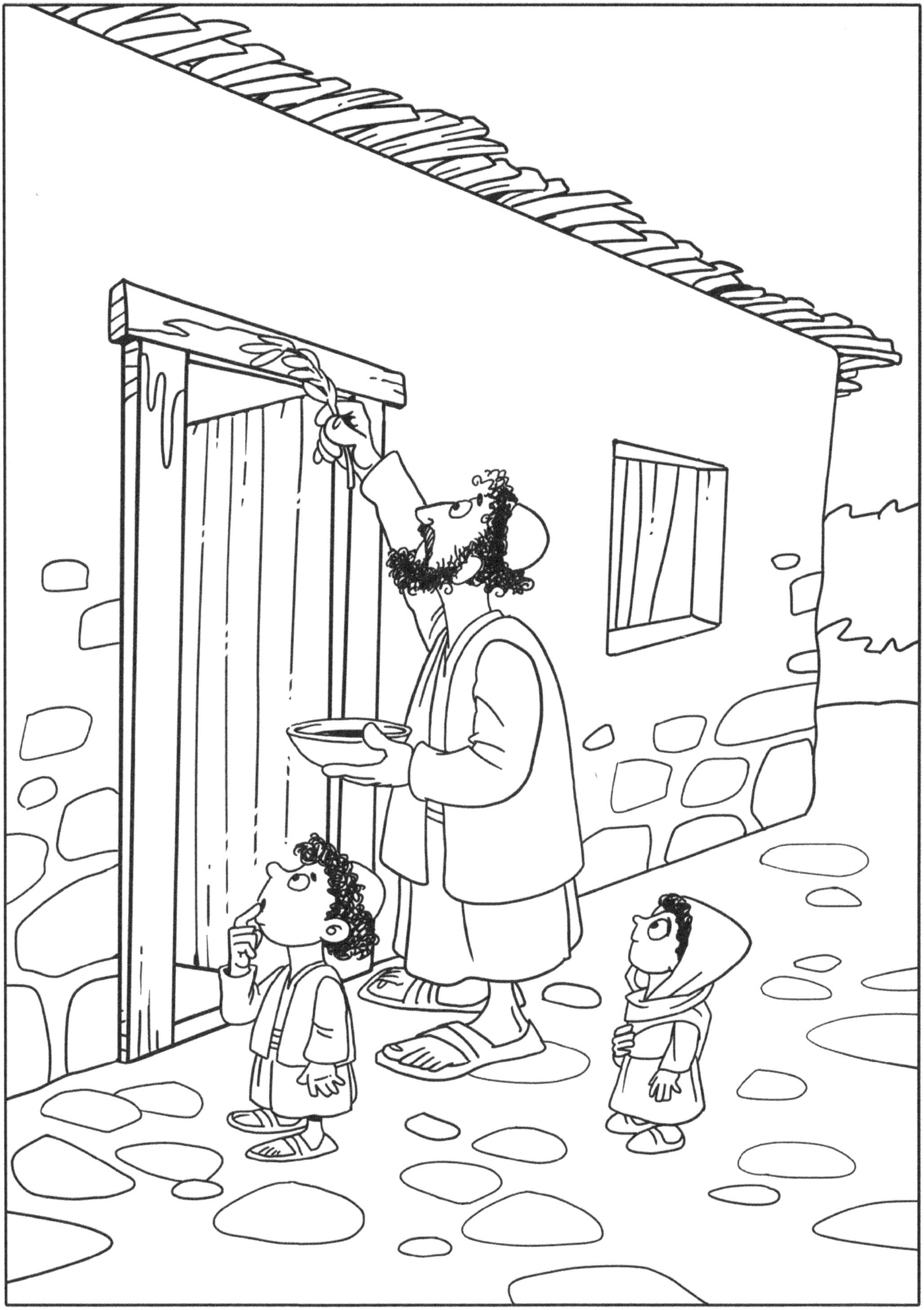

The tenth plague! God kills all the firstborns of Egypt.

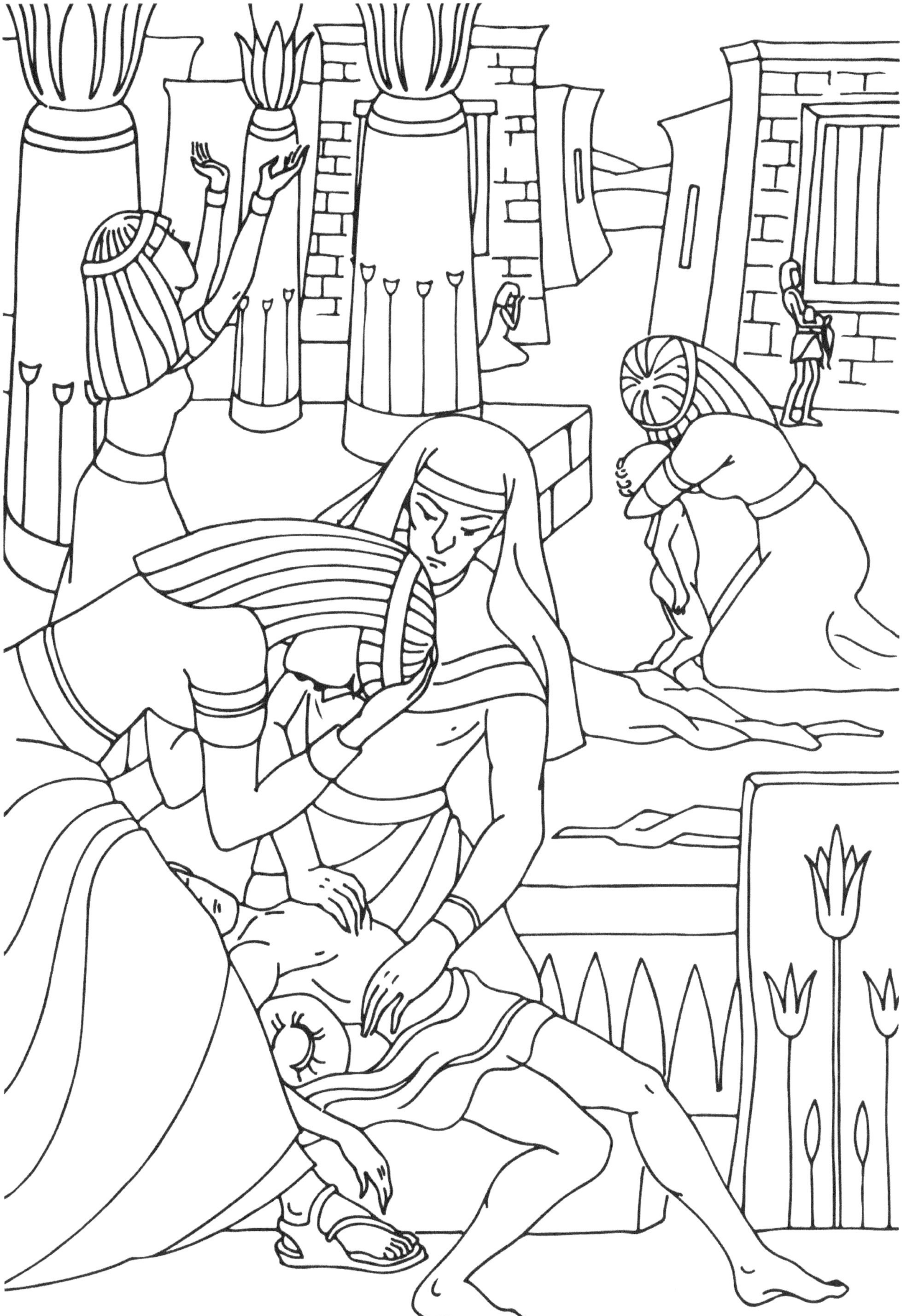

The Israelites need to flee, and there is no time to wait for the dough to rise, so they take bread which is unleavened - Matzot.

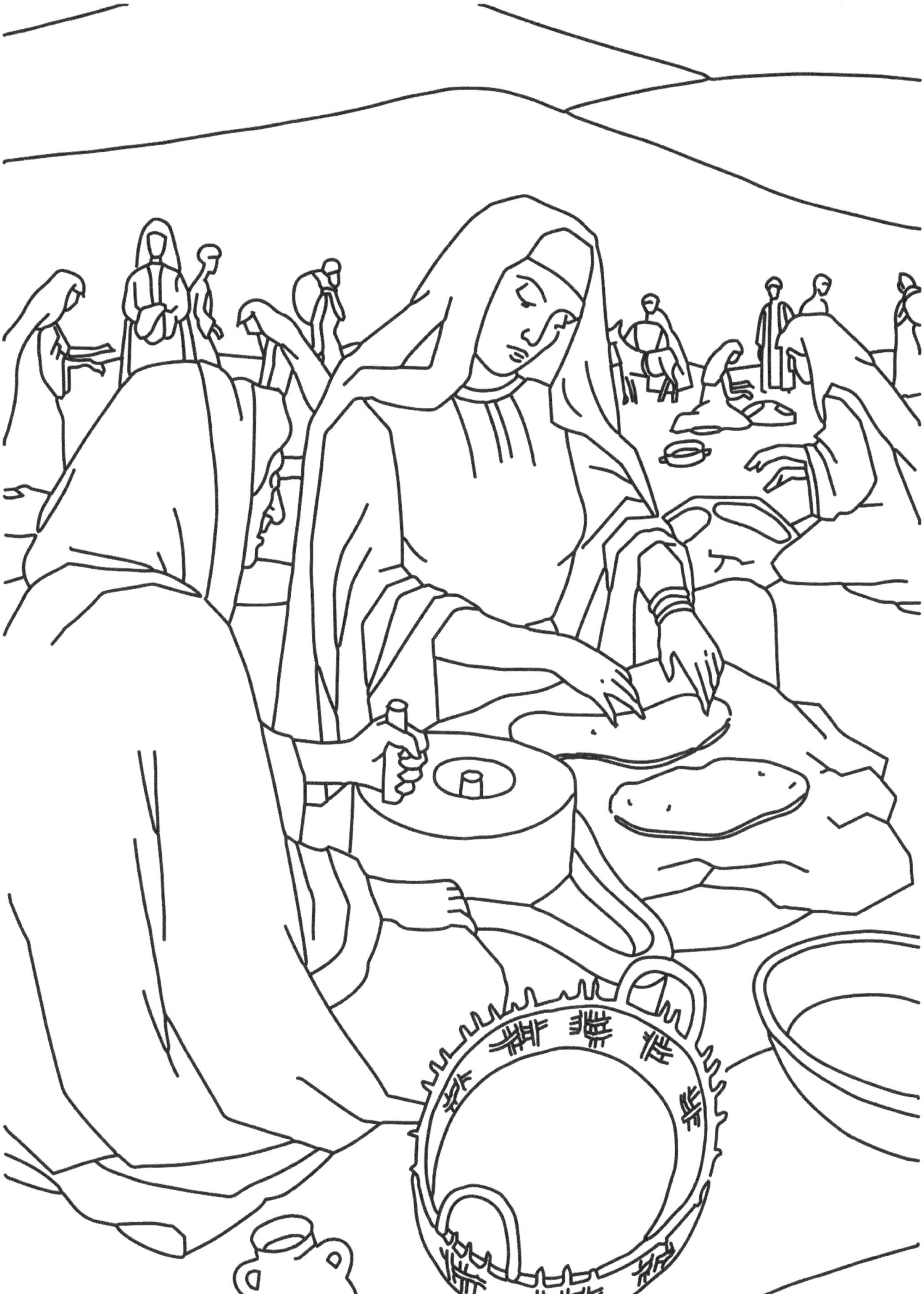

But Pharaoh decides to take is army and chase them. The Children of Israel get trapped with the Red Sea behind them.

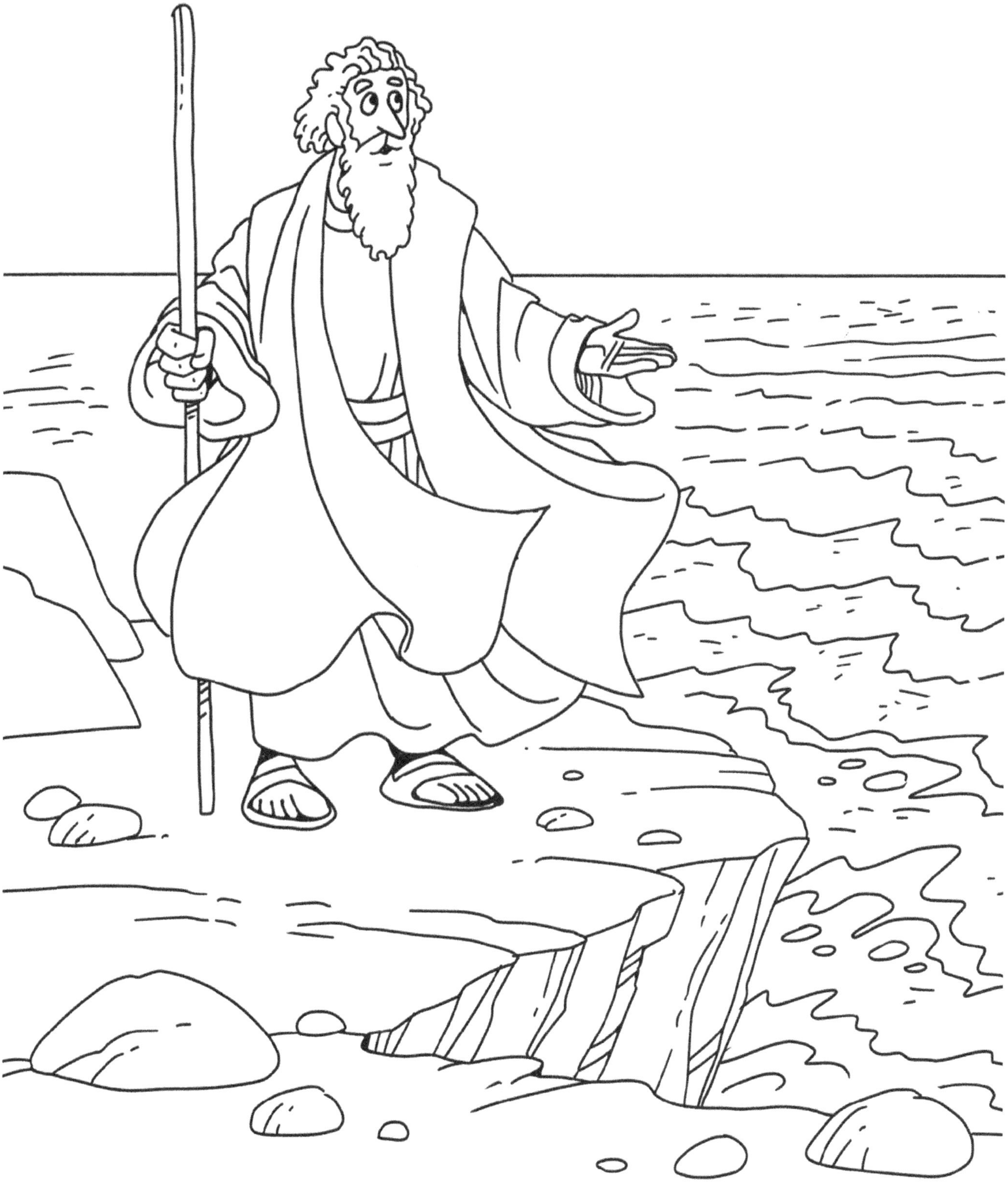

God makes a miracle! He tells Moses to raise his staff and the sea splits into two! The Children of Israel cross on dry land safely.

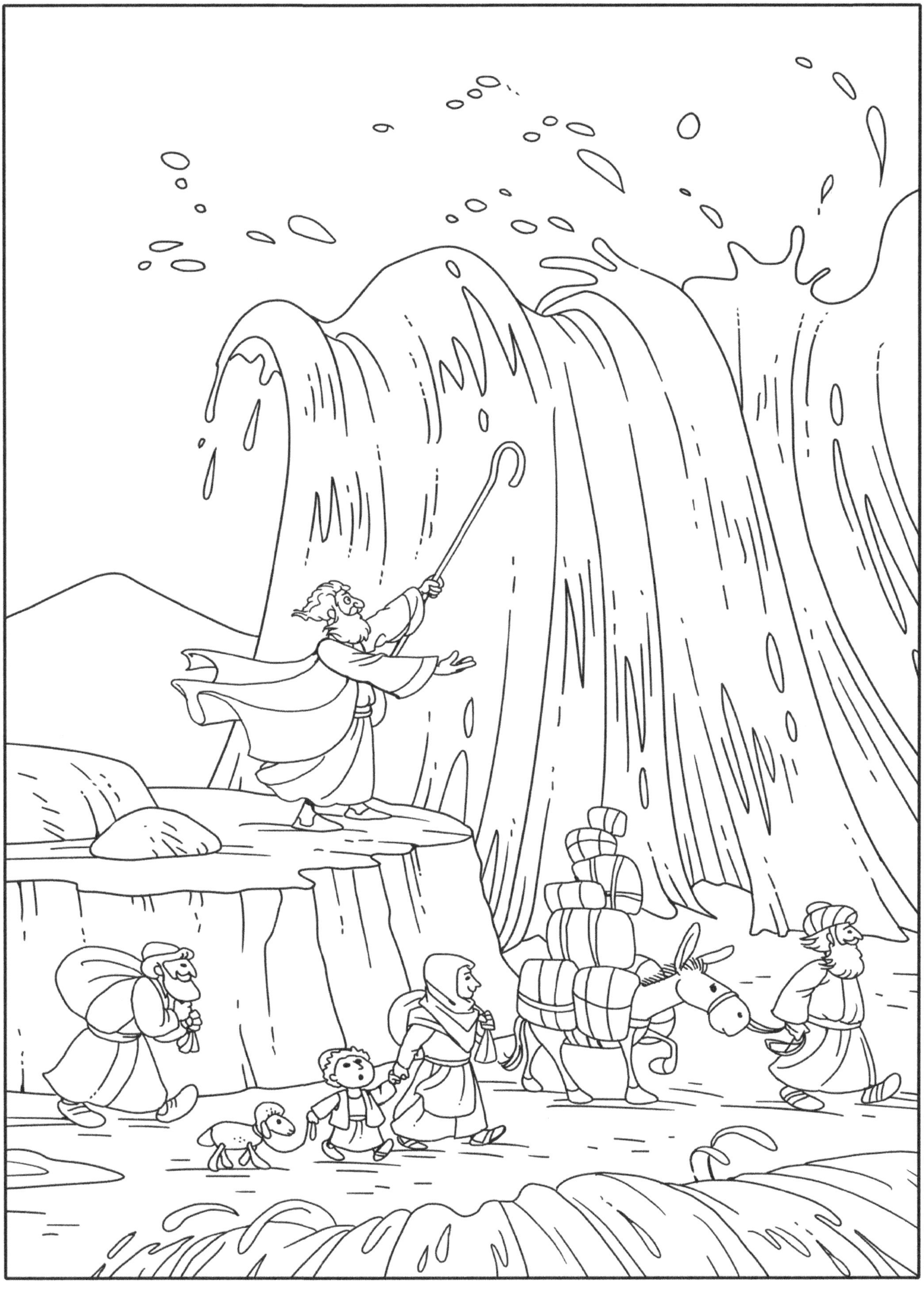

When Moses lowers his staff, the sea closes on Pharaoh's army.

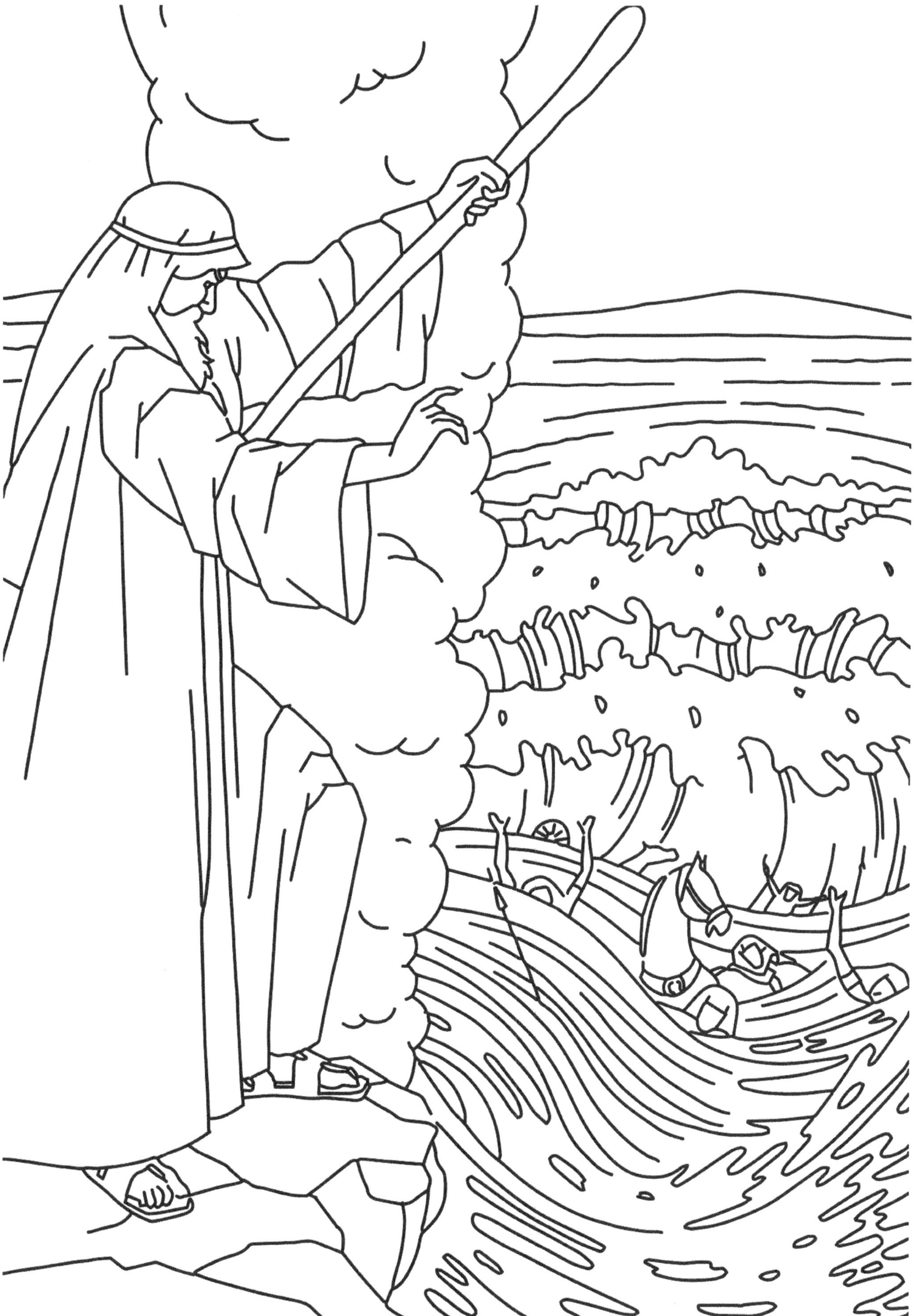

God leads the people all the way to Mt. Sinai!

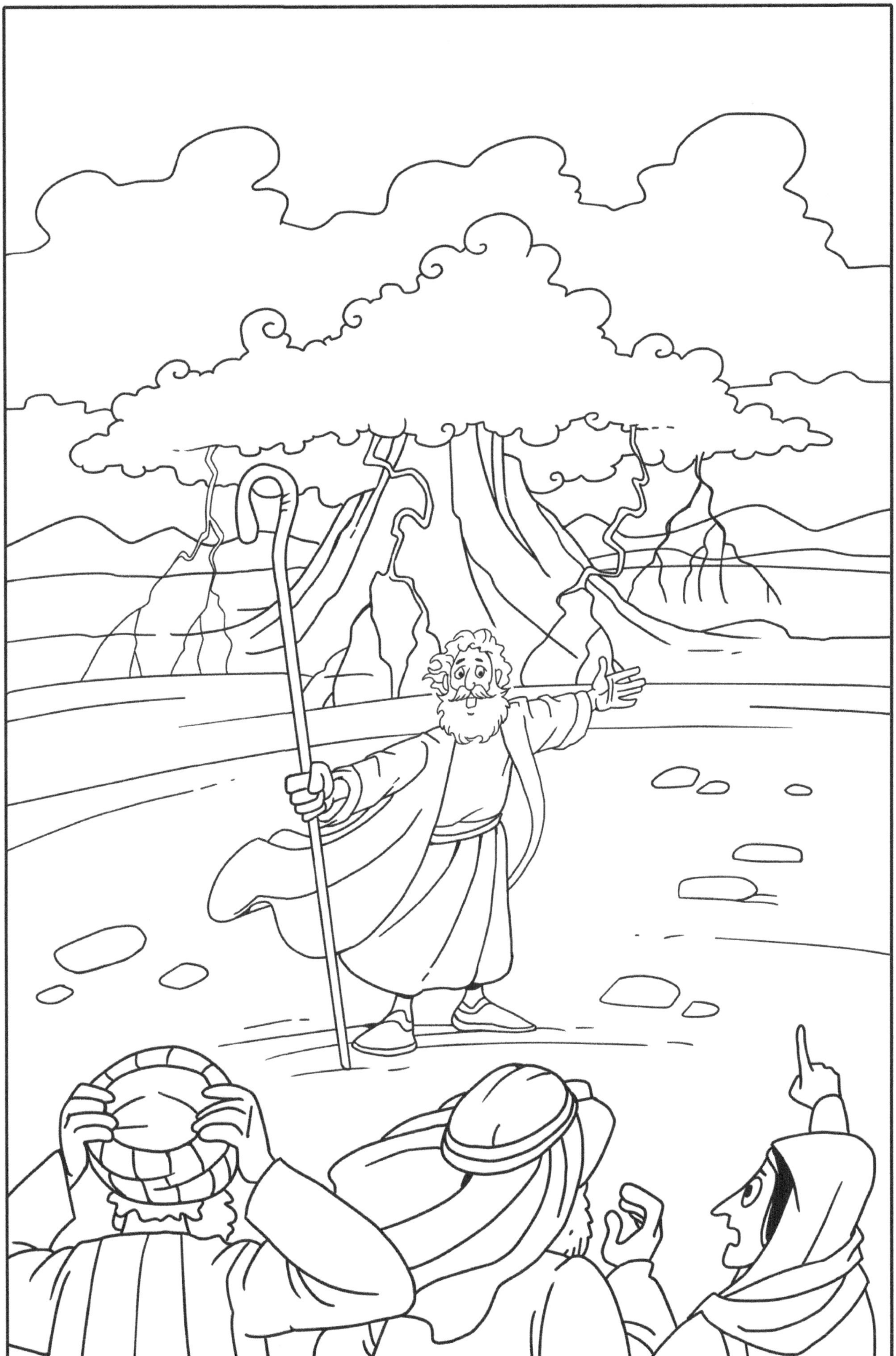

Moses sees the golden idols and breaks the first two Templates.

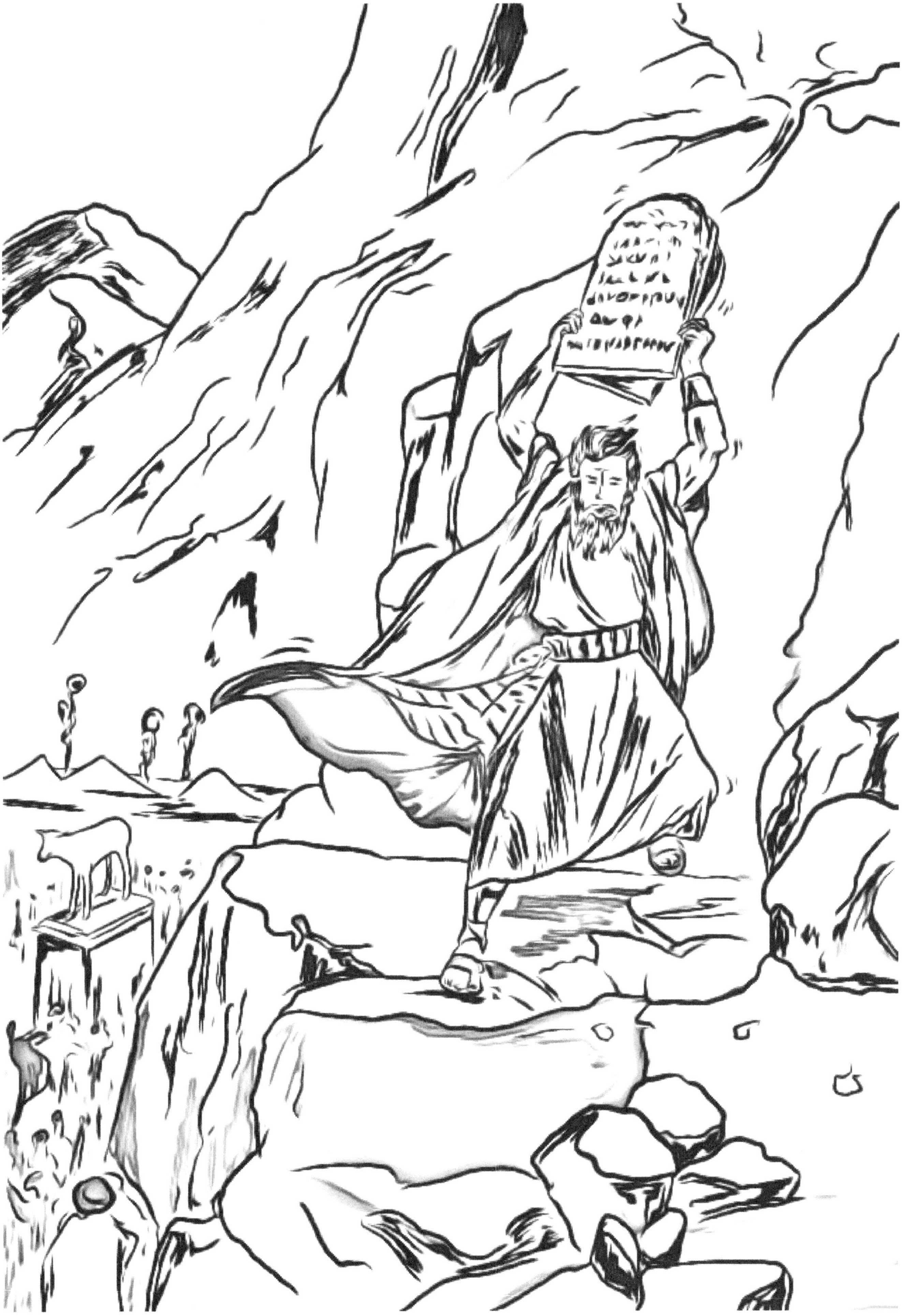

But God loves the Children of Israel and gives them the holy Torah.

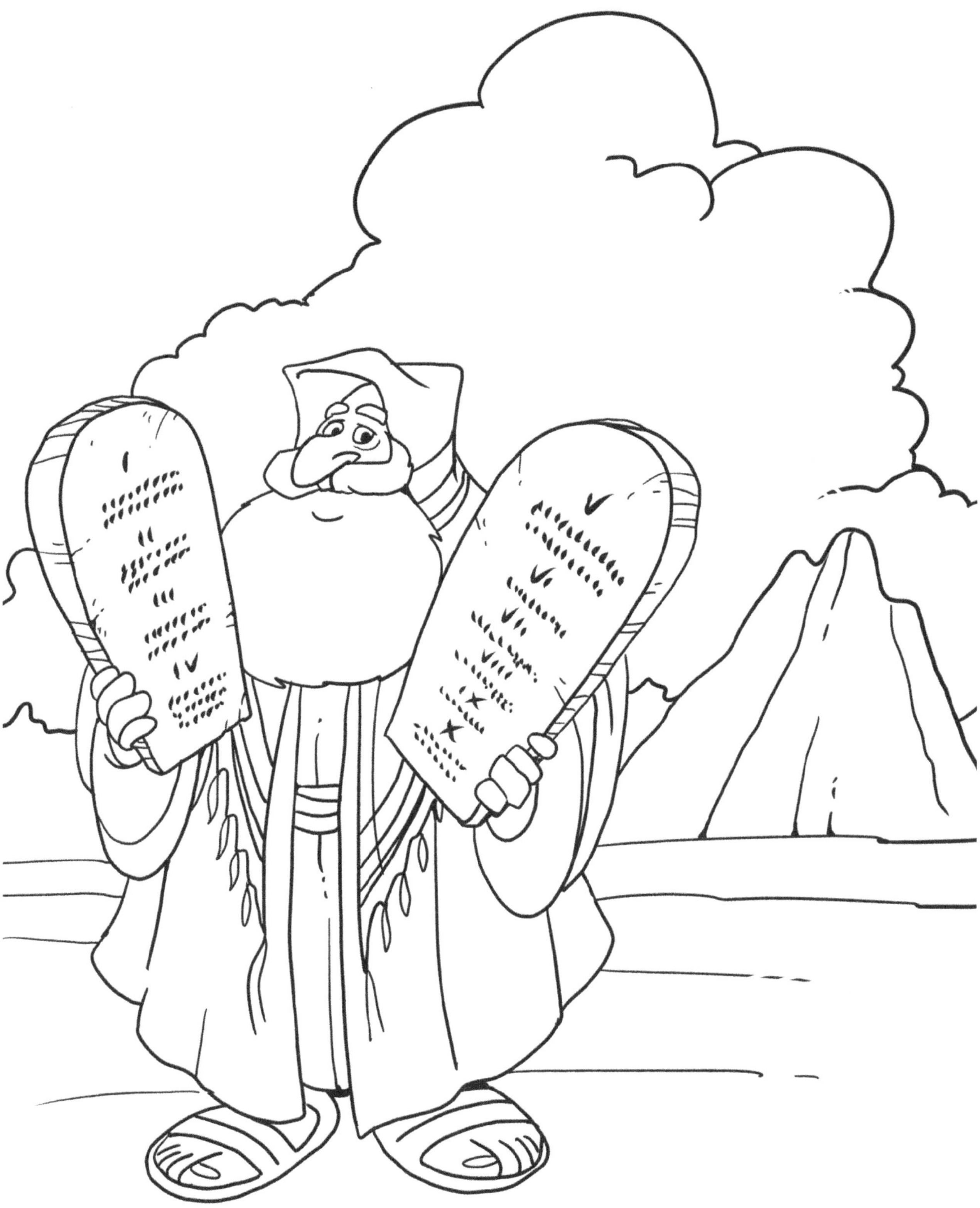

The Children of Israel prepare to go back to their land.

יוסף

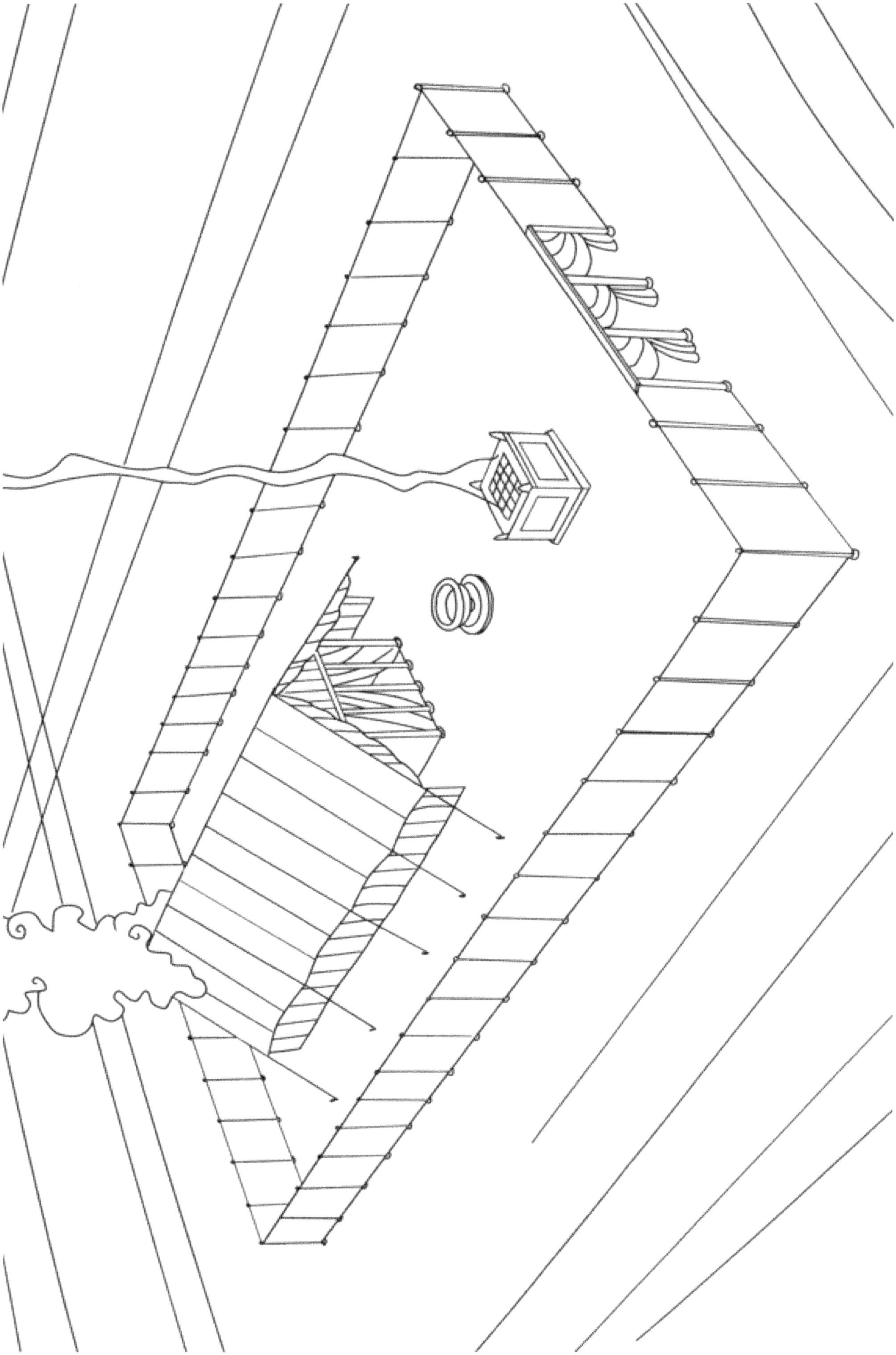

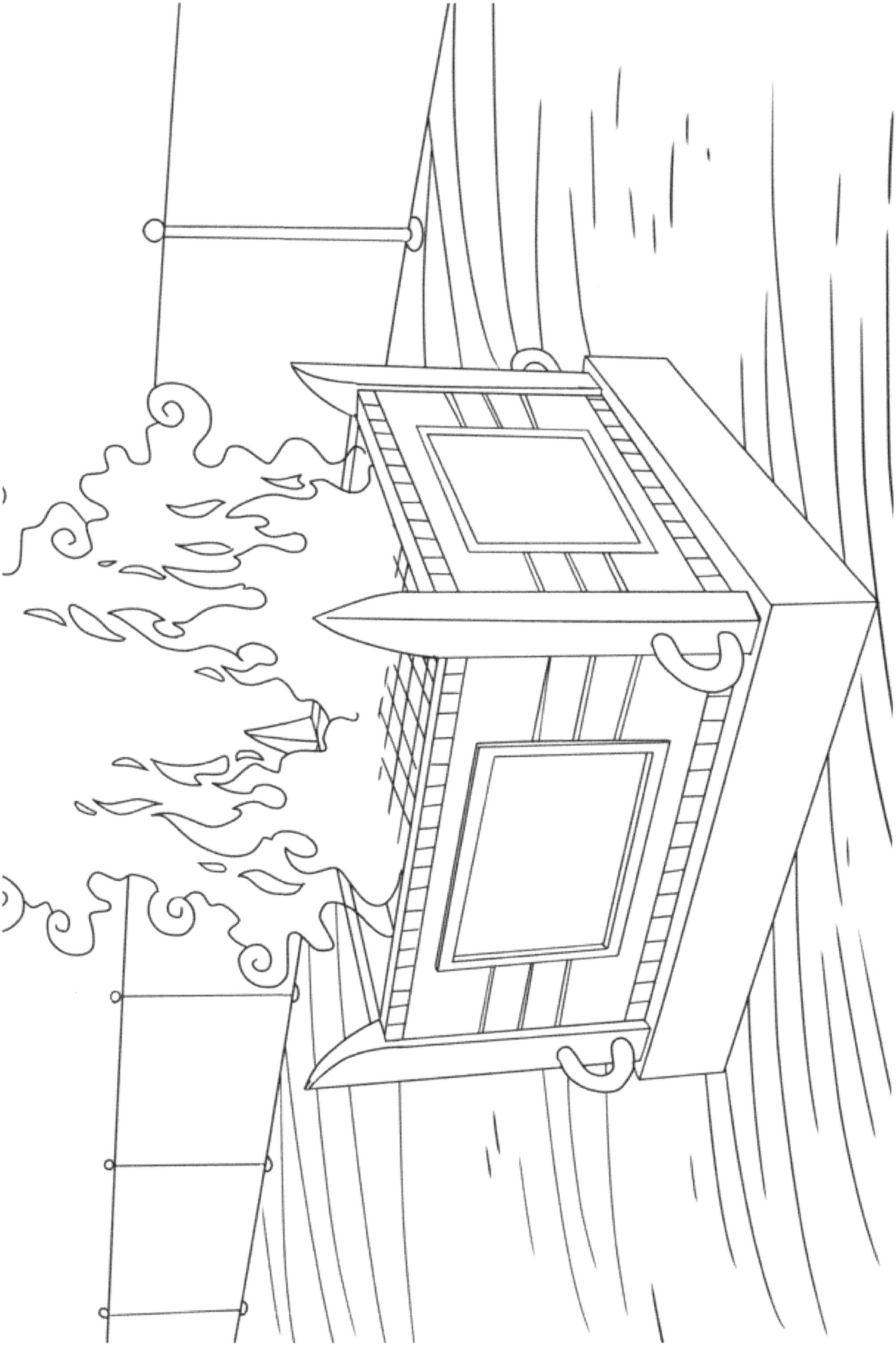

The spies came back and said Israel is a land of Milk and Honey.

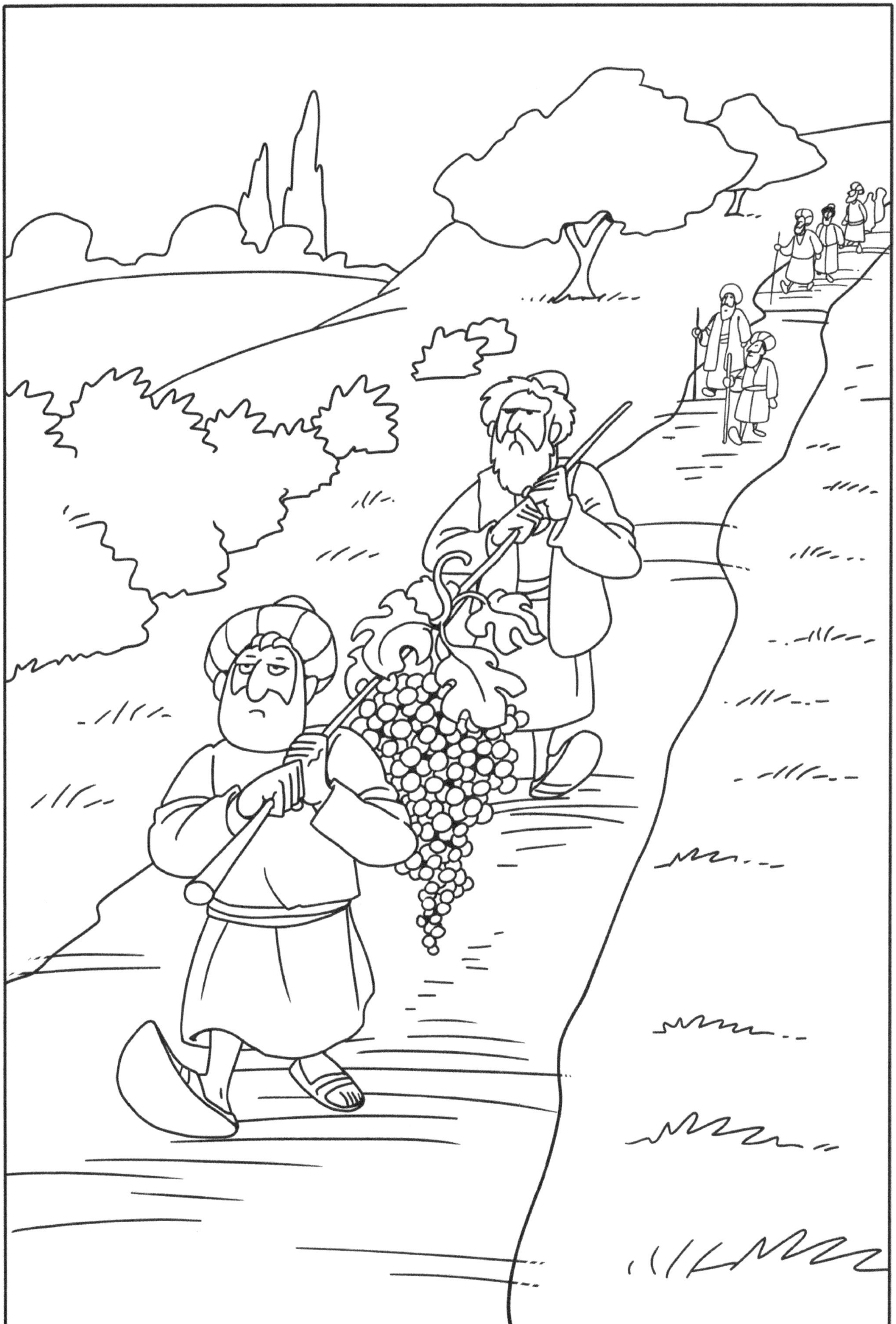

ISRAEL

The Temple Mount in Jerusalem - Where King Solomon build the first Jewish Temple! The first and second Jewish Temples stayed on the Temple Mount for 900 years!

Jerusalem

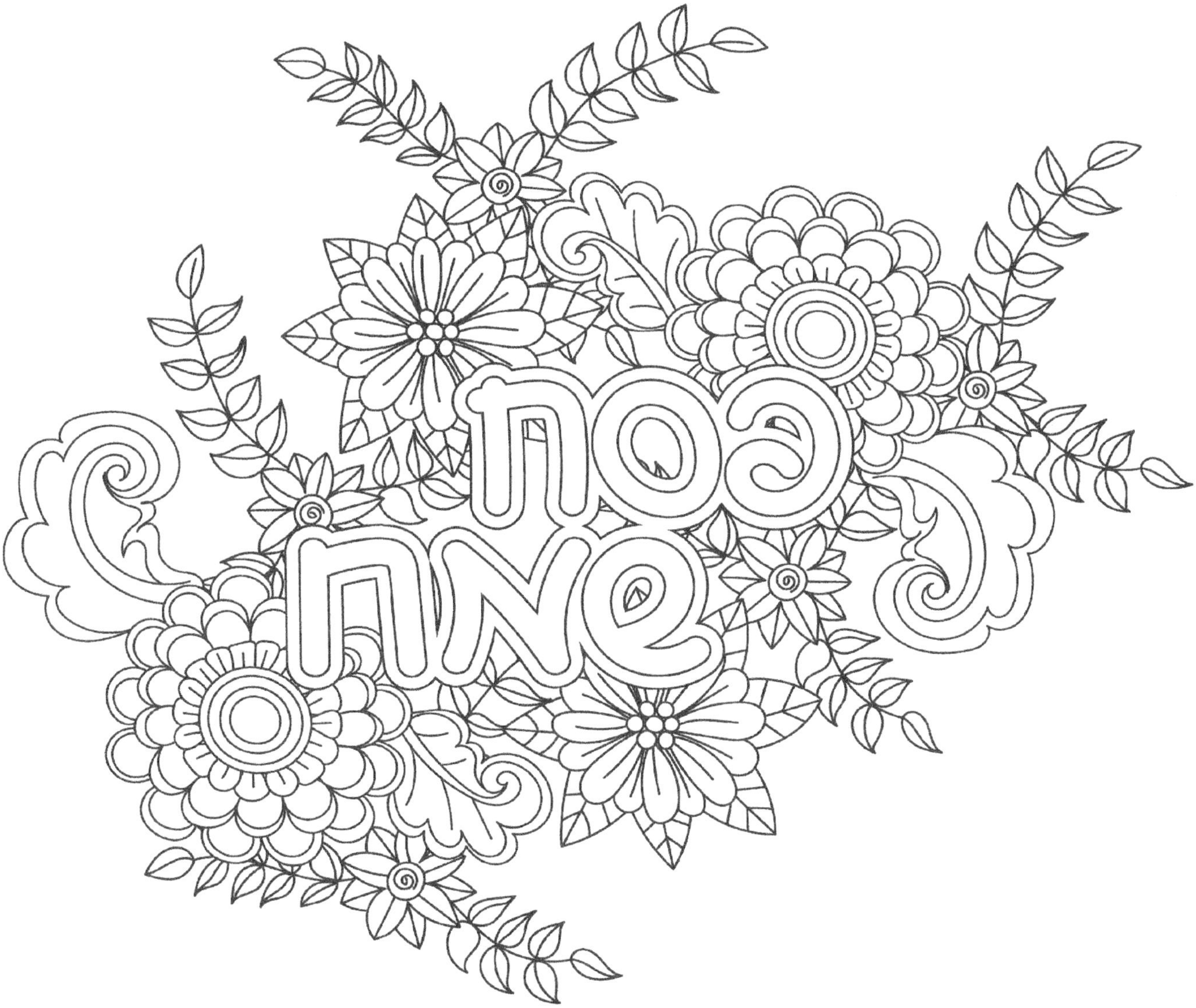
פסח
שמח

GOOD WINE

HAPPY PASSOVER

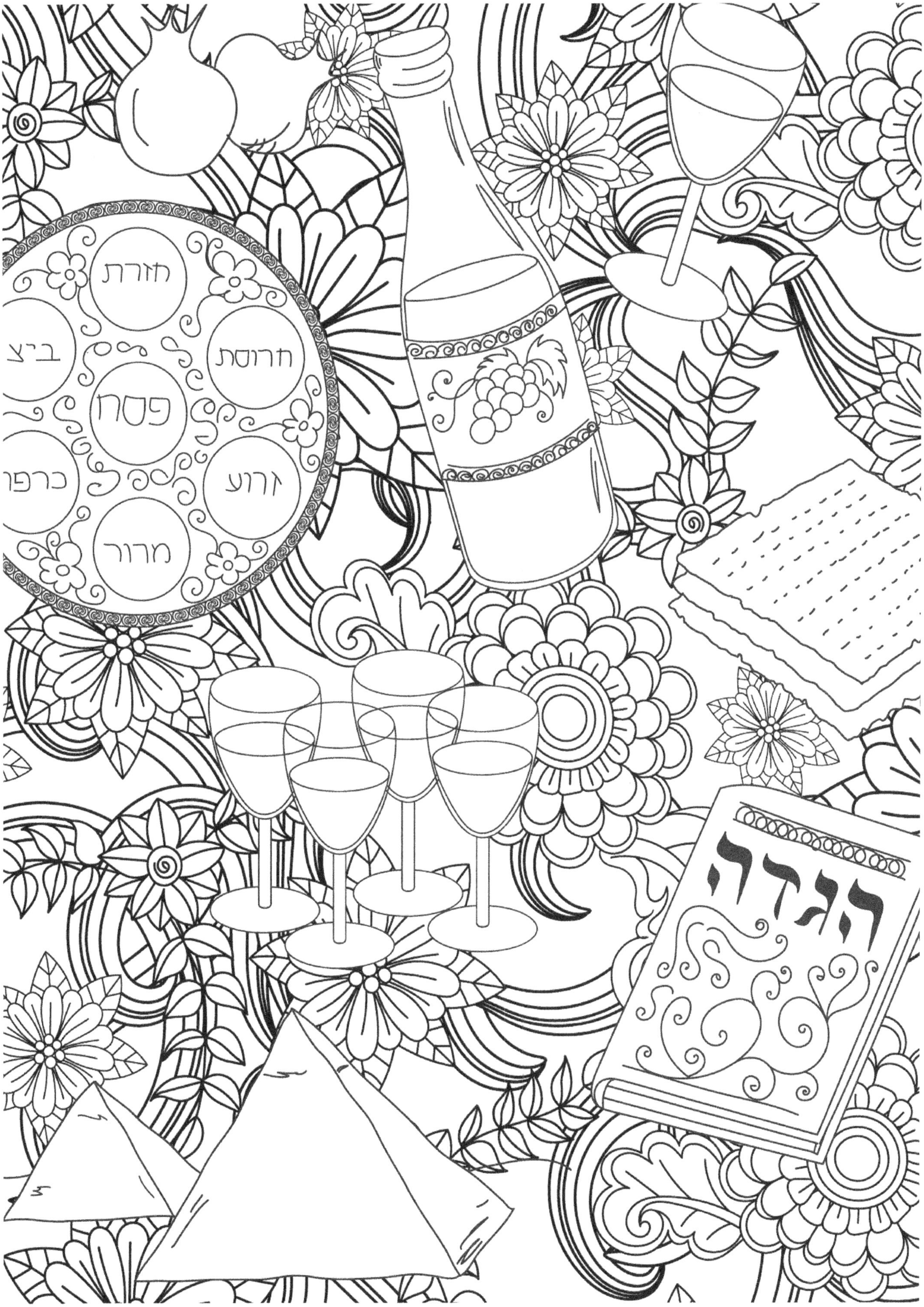
חזרת
חרוסת
פסח
זרוע
מרור
הגדה

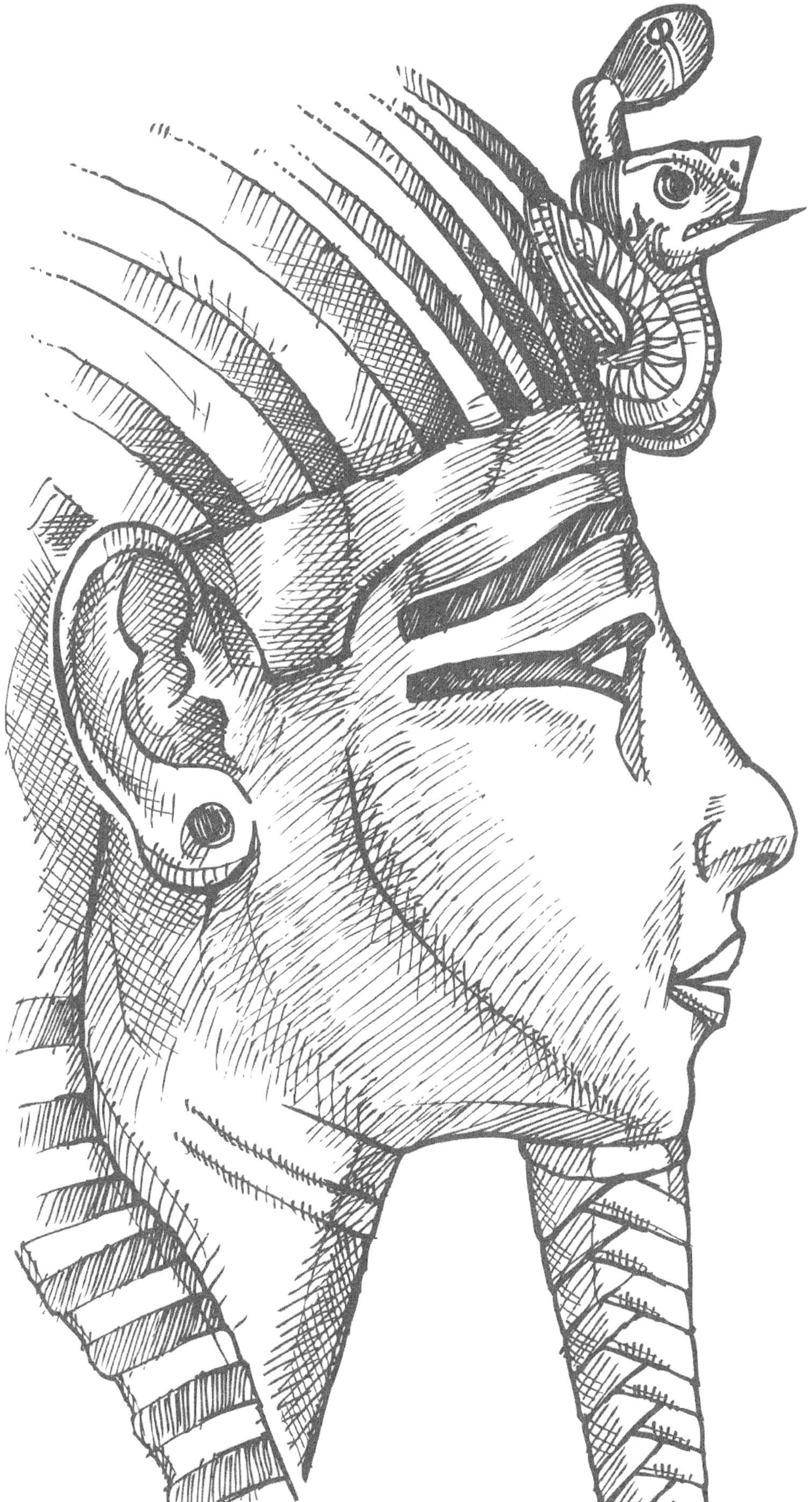

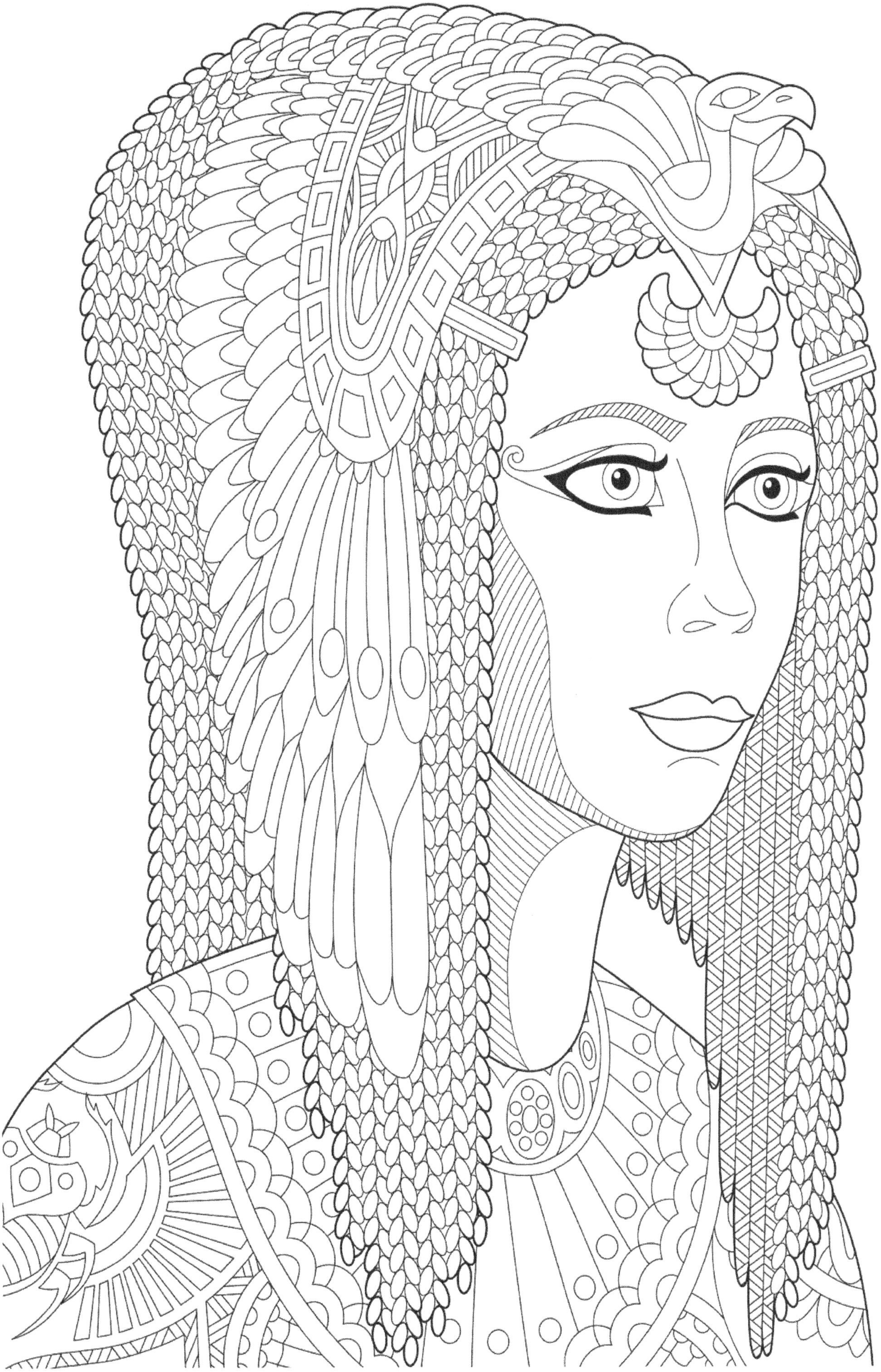

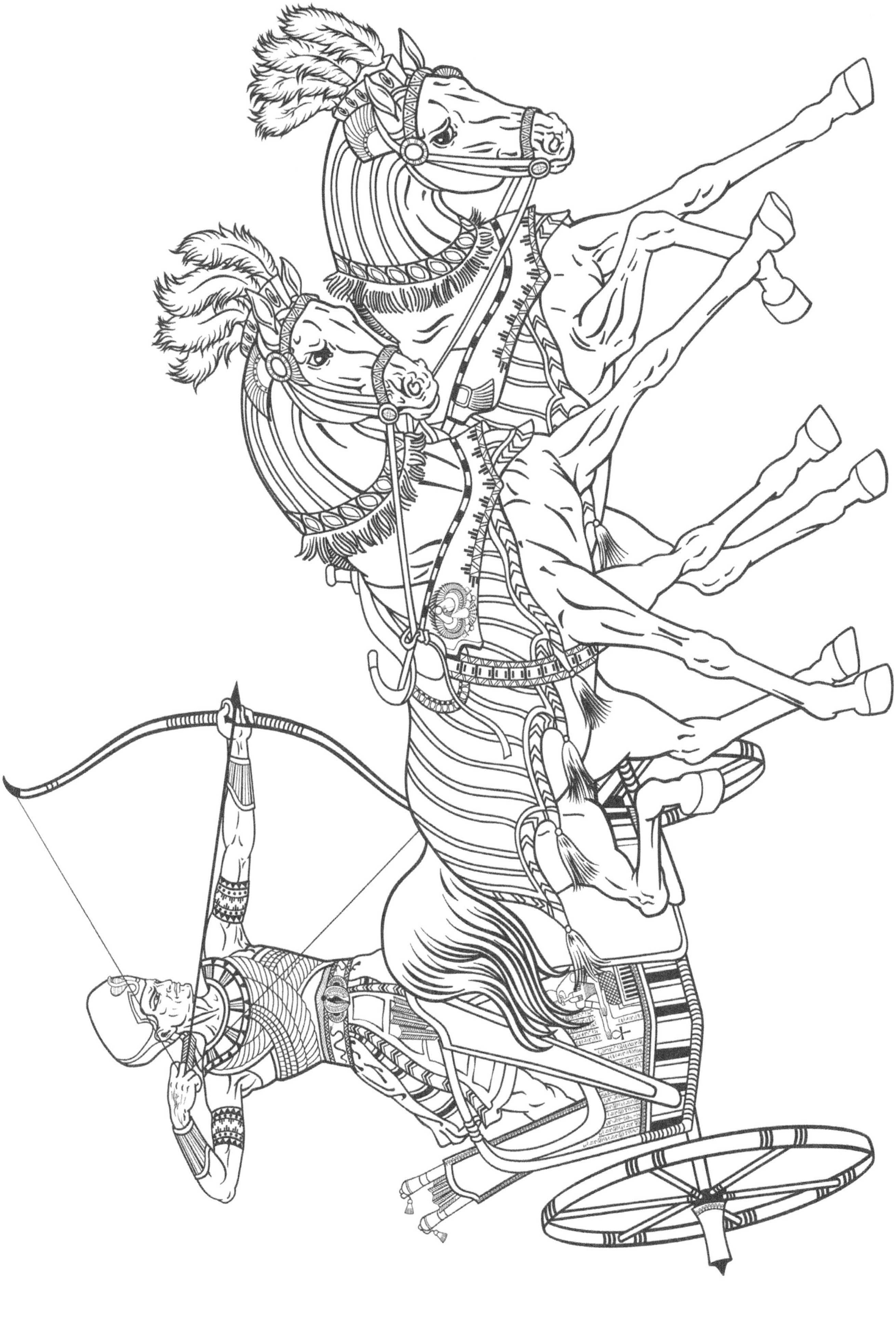

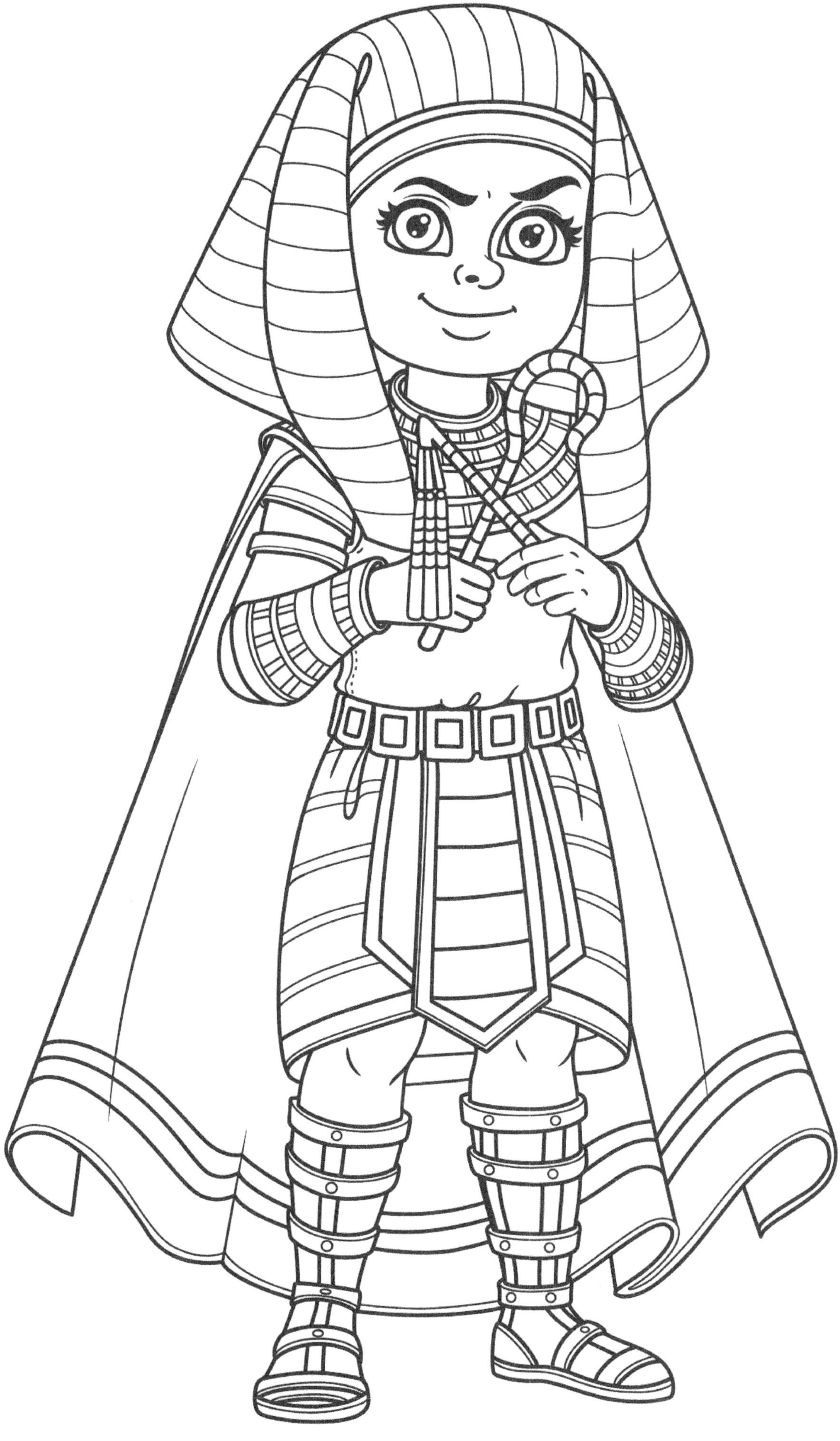

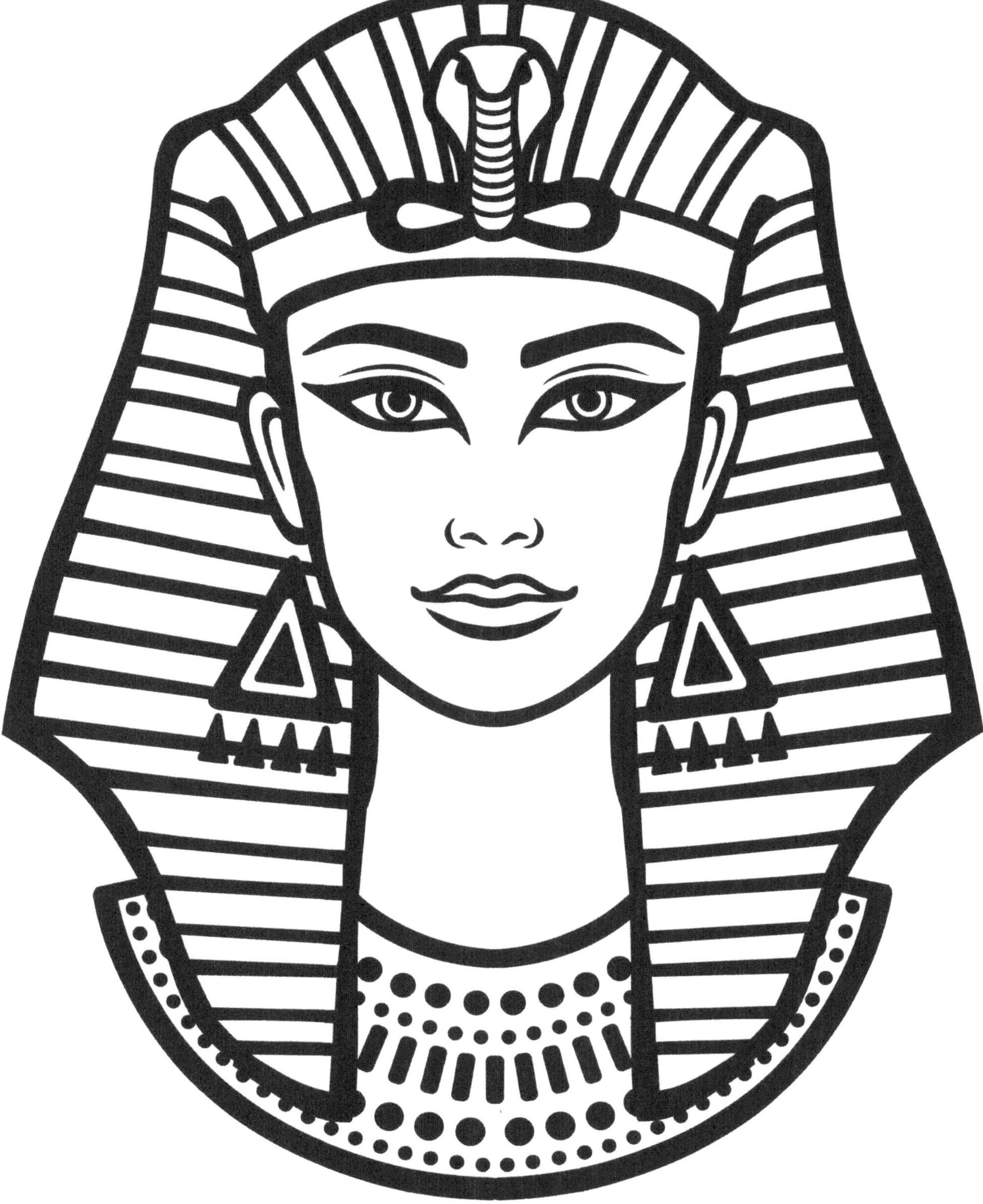

Thank you for coloring with us!
Happy Passover
פסח שמח

More Passover Books For Kids:

Chad Gadya

Passover Story

Rachel Mintz

Passover Story

The Boy Who Helped Moses

Rachel Mintz

Rachel Mintz

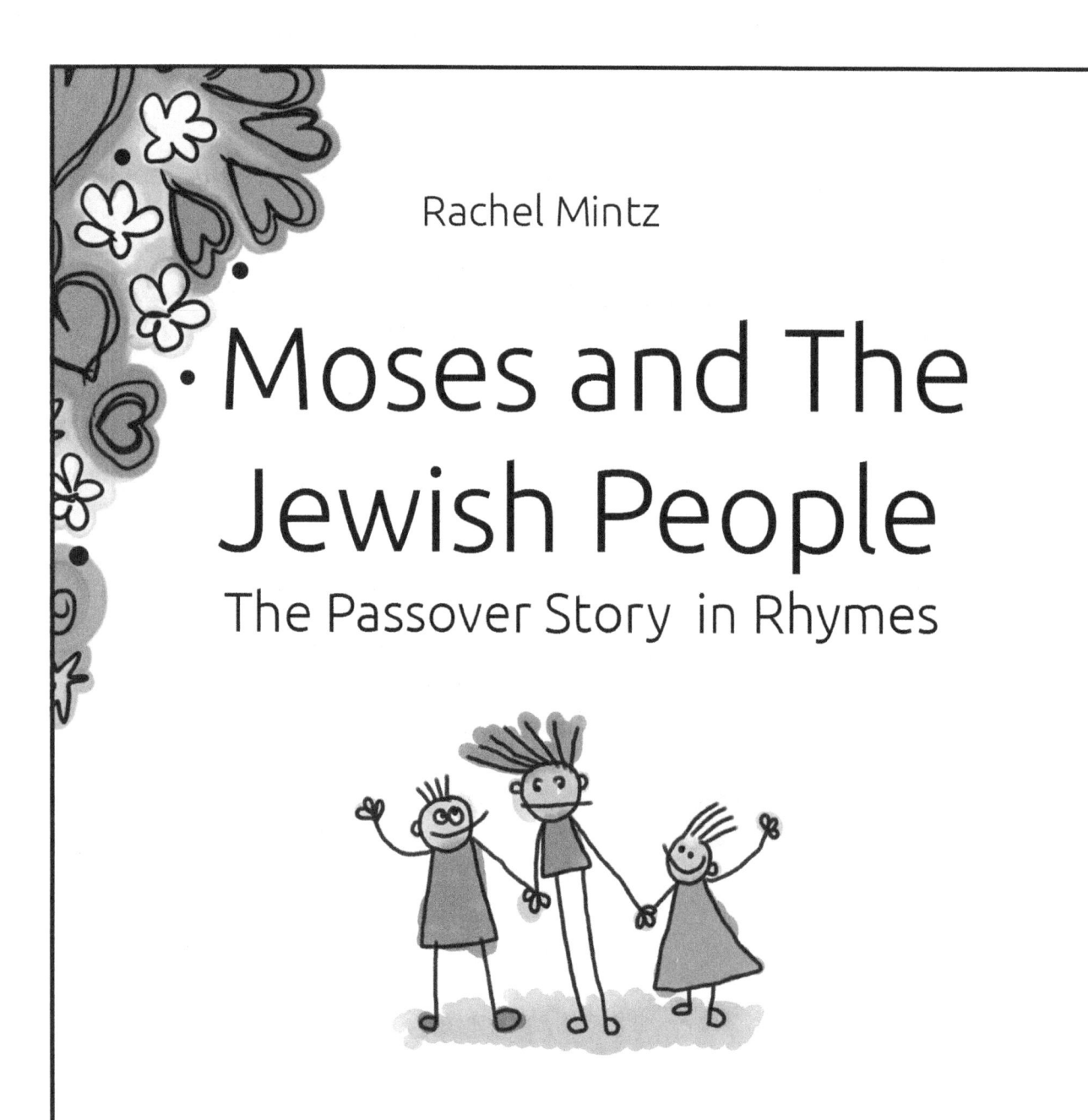

Moses and The Jewish People

The Passover Story in Rhymes

Passover Fun Book For Children

Seder | Haggadah | Afikoman | Moses | Ten Plagues | Chametz | Matzah | Songs

Rachel Mintz & David Levin

Passover Count Book

Rachel Mintz

Learning To Count
1-13 in Hebrew/English

חג שמח